Public Service in Higher Education:
Practices and Priorities

by Patricia H. Crosson

ASHE-ERIC Higher Education Research Report No. 7, 1983

Prepared by

® *Clearinghouse on Higher Education*
The George Washington University

Published by

Association for the Study of Higher Education

Jonathan D. Fife,
Series Editor

Cite as:
Crosson, Patricia H. *Public Service in Higher Education: Practices and Priorities*. ASHE-ERIC Higher Education Research Report No. 7. Washington, D.C.: Association for the Study of Higher Education, 1983.

The ERIC Clearinghouse on Higher Education invites individuals to submit proposals for writing monographs for the Higher Education Research Report series. Proposals must include:
1. A detailed manuscript proposal of not more than five pages.
2. A 75-word summary to be used by several review committees for the initial screening and rating of each proposal.
3. A vita.
4. A writing sample.

ISSN 0737-1292
ISBN 0-913317-06-3

ERIC° Clearinghouse on Higher Education
The George Washington University
One Dupont Circle, Suite 630
Washington, D.C. 20036

Association for the Study of Higher Education
One Dupont Circle, Suite 630
Washington, D.C. 20036

This publication was partially prepared with funding from the National Institute of Education, U.S. Department of Education, under contract no. 400-82-0011. The opinions expressed in this report do not necessarily reflect the positions or policies of NIE or the Department.

WITHDRAWN

JUN 4 1985

Richard Lonsdale
Professor of Educational Administration
New York University

Linda Kock Lorimer
Associate General Counsel
Yale University

Virginia B. Nordby
Director
Affirmative Action Programs
University of Michigan

Eugene Oliver
Director, University Office of School & College Relations
University of Illinois—Champaign

Harold Orlans
Lawyer

Marianne Phelps
Assistant Provost for Affirmative Action
The George Washington University

Gary K. Probst
Professor of Reading
Prince Georges Community College

Cliff Sjogren
Director of Admissions
University of Michigan

Al Smith
Assistant Director of the Institute of Higher Education &
    Professor of Instructional Leadership & Support
University of Florida

CONTENTS

FOREWORD

Higher Education has been described as the curator, creator and critic of knowledge. To fulfill this multiple role, higher education has devoted itself to teaching, research, and public service. teaching, the curatorial process, preserves knowledge by passing it from one generation to another. Research (and subsequent publications) serves as curator, creator, and critic by articulating what is known, expanding the knowledge-base through new discoveries, and carefully examining the old and new. Public service represents a further extension of academe's curator role. Through public service, higher education institutions enable society to use knowledge more effectively.

Other factors also make legitimate higher education's involvement in public service. Altruistically, higher education has a responsibility to be involved with public service because of its unique position of being the center of knowledge; it has an obligation to share its knowledge with more than its own students and faculty. From the position of intellectual self-interest, public service provides a laboratory for testing current knowledge. Putting knowledge into practice permits discovery of what is still unknown, what works and what does not. Finally higher education is obligated to help society as a repayment for its financial support. Because both private and public institutions receive direct and indirect tax support, they have a responsibility for more than just teaching students and conducting research.

While there is an acceptance, at least in principle, of higher education's involvement with public service, many barriers inhibit the fulfillment of this mission: (1) Individual faculty members are not generally rewarded for their public service; publishing and teaching normally receive the greatest peer recognition and promotion/salary support. This is due partly to the perception that public service is not part of the intellectual process of higher education. (2) The mission of public service is not well defined by the institution and therefore not built into the reward system. (3) Institutions are reluctant to spread their already scarce resources beyond what they consider their primary functions, teaching and research. (4) There is a concern that many public service activities may be seen as politically partisan, indirectly (e.g., social and environmental issues) or directly (e.g., serving an administration dominated by one political party).

This Research Report by Patricia H. Crosson, Associate Professor of Higher Education and Director of the Institute for Higher Education at the University of Pittsburgh, reexamines the literatue concerned with public service. It concentrates on service to community, state and local governments, and business and industry. Because of space limitations and the changing nature of priorities, service to the federal government is not reviewed.

Dr. Crosson's concluding chapters outline ways to organize for public service she offers useful guidelines to administrators and faculty members trying to balance out the mission of their institution in relationship to its available resources.

Jonathan D. Fife
Director and Series Editor
ERIC Clearinghouse on Higher Education
The George Washington University

EXECUTIVE SUMMARY

Service has long been a distinctive part of higher education in the United States. Most administrators and faculty members would identify service as one of the three major functions of their institution. They would describe with rhetorical flourish countless programs and projects in service to society. Most of these same administrators and faculty members would also say, however, that service is quite a distant third after teaching and research and that institutional priorities and reward systems—unwritten yet well known—operate against service in higher education. The questionable priority and doubtful reward value are especially apparent when the "service" is public service for individuals and groups external to the campus rather than service to the academic discipline or to the institution.

Is Public Service an Important Function?

The subject of college and university public service involves an ongoing debate about its role and importance in higher education—a debate that is inextricably linked to fundamental questions about the nature and purposes of higher education. Different perspectives on the nature and purposes of higher education are revealed through three popular metaphors—ivory tower, social service station, and culture mart (Adelman 1973). Each concept of higher education is characterized by a different definition of service and differing perspectives on the nature of service and its role and function in higher education. Service can be provided through the fulfillment of teaching and research, through "ideas of value," through social criticism, through social problem solving, or through social activism. Each form of service has its advocates in the historical and contemporary literature.

Throughout the history of higher education in the United States, the concept of service and references to service have been used to justify claims for public support. Often service in this sense is taken to mean the fulfillment of teaching and research. Charles William Eliot asked rhetorically in his 1869 inaugural address at Harvard:

> *And what will the University do for the community? First, it will make a rich return of learning, poetry and piety. Secondly, it will foster the sense of public duty—that great virtue which makes republics possible* (Hofstader and Smith 1961, p. 263).

Most . . . administrators and faculty members would . . . say . . . that service is quite a distant third after teaching and research . . .

The concept of service, linked with notions of utility, has also been used throughout our history to justify and rationalize new departures in higher education. From the expansion of the classical curriculum to include scientific studies to the creation of land grant colleges, professional schools, interdisciplinary institutes and centers, and recent programs of technology transfer, we have made the case that each new endeavor was necessary as a service to society.

The ideal of public service was perhaps best captured by Andrew S. Draper in a 1907 commencement address:

The American university will carry the benefits of scientific research to the doors of the multitude. It will make healthier houses and handsomer streets, richer farms and safer railways, happier towns and thriftier cities, through the application of fundamental principles to all the activities of all the people (p. 41).

The missionary overtones and the zeal of Draper's rhetoric pervade discussions of service throughout the literature and can be found in much contemporary writing, but Derek Bok (1982) captures somewhat better the current tone of the debate:

By 1970, then, the issues were clearly defined. Should universities turn inward and dedicate themselves to learning and research for their own sake, benefiting society indirectly through advances in basic knowledge and the education of able students? Should they continue instead to respond energetically to society's requests for new services, new training programs, and new forms of expert advice? Or should they take the initiative and set their own agenda for reform by deciding for themselves which programs to mount and which projects to encourage in order to bring about social change? (p. 66).

During the decades between Presidents Draper and Bok, we have abandoned the zealous notion that higher education can be all things to all people and have returned to ask, as President Eliot did in 1869, what services can or should higher education perform for the community. Each of the choices Bok poses as questions has many advocates, and each continues to be defended in the name of public service.

It is unlikely, however, that single "yes" or "no" answers to these questions will be formulated for higher education as a whole or for any college or university. The debate over the social responsibility of the university is a continuing debate.

What Services Should We Perform?
While we have debated the issues of the role and function of service in higher education, we have been engaged in extensive and various service activities. We have offered noncredit community service programs responsive to every conceivable educational need and interest from basic English to belly dancing. We have made our facilities available for and helped sponsor cultural and civic activities. We have developed special training programs for business and industry and for local and state government employees. We have created extension programs, technical assistance centers, and other special units to help solve specific social and policy problems. We have been engaged in research services through contractual arrangements and consulting for every conceivable external agency. All of these areas and more are college and university public service activities.

Draper's ideal has been most fully realized by Clark Kerr's multiversity, but all types of colleges and universities are involved in public service. Service activities differ across types of institutions—public or private, two-year or four-year colleges and universities—and among institutions of the same type. The easiest way to categorize public service, however, is by external recipient: service to the community, service to state and local governments, service to business and industry.

Community service is especially important for community colleges. Community colleges have developed exciting programs and activities, and the literature contains an interesting debate over the extent to which community service is or should be the major function of the community college. Many state universities are experimenting with new offices and programs intended to link their institutions more closely to the legislative and executive branches of state and local government. Formal research partnerships have been developed between public and private research universities and major corporations to foster the immediate application of scientific breakthroughs to new products and economic developments.

We continue to debate the issue of what services are best and most appropriately performed by colleges and universities. At the same time, we continue to innovate, to develop model programs and practices, and to experiment with new approaches to the delivery of service.

How Should We Organize for Public Service?

The problem for college and university administrators and faculty becomes one of making choices and decisions. How should a particular institution define itself in relation to society? Should we assume a variety of social responsibilities and make public service something more than an added dimension in higher education? What specific organizational structures, personnel policies, and financial mechanisms will clarify the role and function of public service and enable service to be performed effectively?

The literature on service in higher education provides no easy answers to these questions. Although it includes little in the way of formal research results and evaluation, it does reveal how some institutions have answered these questions and contains many ideas worthy of close examination. Many institutions have developed formal policy statements of public service. Others have created high-level offices or other special units to coordinate service activities. Still others have experimented with ways of documenting and assessing service for decisions about personnel. Some state and local governments have provided specific resources for service activities beyond those targeted for research and teaching; others expect services for free. Perhaps the most difficult, as well as the most enduring, question of public service is the question of how we can afford it—or indeed whether we can afford not to do it.

INTRODUCTION

Service is a word widely used in higher education. It is rarely defined, yet it has many different meanings and connotations. For many it is a rhetorical device. It is always employed to help justify the use of resources and appears even more prominently in the budget requests of public institutions. Independent institutions have begun to emphasize service as the question of support for diversity and choice through the preservation of the private sector becomes an issue of public policy. Service is also used to rationalize new initiatives, new degree programs, and new professional schools and to describe a vast array of activities in colleges and universities.

Why, then, make yet another attempt to grapple with the issue of service? Why risk the tendency to rhetoric that inevitably seems to accompany such discussions in the literature? The only answer is that service is important to higher education. Although usually considered a distant third behind teaching and research, service is commonly listed among the three major missions and functions of higher education. An enormous amount of activity is justified and undertaken under the banner of service. As colleges and universities face new and uncertain futures, it is tempting to promise ever new levels of services but exceedingly risky to do so without examining the implications and the consequences.

Three broad categories of activities have come to be labeled service:

- *college or university service:* committee or other governance activities internal to the department, college, school, or campus related to program development and institutional policy
- *professional service:* committee, editorial, or other work for national or regional professional associations and/or academic disciplines
- *public service:* activities "other than" basic research and teaching involving direct relationships with groups external to the academic community.

This research report focuses on public service in American colleges and universities.

The subject of service and the use of the concept is by no means new in higher education. In the United States, it has been inextricably linked with large, complex questions of the nature, purposes, and priorities of higher education and of the relationship between higher education and society. Definitions of public service, attitudes about its role and function in higher education, even preferences for forms and types of service activities and service recipients, are shaped by definitions, attitudes, and preferences concerning education as a whole.

The first chapter discusses rival concepts of higher education and related concepts of public service by examining the definitions of service implicit in three metaphors commonly used to characterize the "nature" of colleges and universities: ivory tower, social service station, and culture mart. It also examines four different perspectives on the question of how the public service mission is best fulfilled: through "ideas of value" (Martin 1977), social criticism, social problem solving, or social activism. The "ideal" of public service is traced historically through examination of the relationship between early colleges, their colonies, and state governments; the movement for curricular reform; and the concept of utility, the land grant era, and the "Wisconsin Idea."

This definition of public service—that which is "other than" basic research and teaching and involves relationships with external groups—while common and useful as a starting point, does not hold up under careful scrutiny. Many of the activities carried out under the banner of public service are research activities; many others are teaching activities. It is often argued that the best form of service is that which most closely resembles teaching and research. What differentiates "public" service activities from other research and teaching activities is that they are performed for groups that have not traditionally been involved with higher education. The concept of what comprises "external" groups changes over time. It is therefore necessary to continually redefine public service in terms of the current dynamics of institutional-societal relationships.

A definition adequate to the current context of higher education includes three major areas:

- *advice, information, and technical assistance to business, government, neighborhood groups, and*

*individuals on problems which the University has
competence to assist in solving;*

- *research toward the solution of public policy problems,
whether by individual or groups of faculty members or
by the formal institutes and centers of the University;*
- *conferences, institutes, seminars, workshops, short
courses, and other nondegree-oriented upgrading and
training for government officials, social service personnel, various professional people, business executives,
and so on* (University of Massachusetts 1971, p. 90).

This definition covers the range of possible service
activities—including research and teaching services—and
the range of potential beneficiaries of college and university
public service.

While public service can be categorized many possible
ways, the following chapters are organized by recipient—
service to communities, service to state and local governments, and service to business and industry.[1] Each of these
types of service involves distinct issues and patterns of
activity, and each is reflected in an identifiable strand of
literature. Each type of activity is undertaken to some
degree by all types of colleges and universities, but community colleges are the major force in community service, state
universities are the primary providers of service to state and
local government, and research universities, both public
and independent, have become the major actors in new
patterns of providing service for business and industry.

The purpose of the first four chapters of this research
report, then, is to provide college and university administrators and faculty members with a review of the major controversies related to the mission of public service in colleges
and universities and with state-of-the-art information
concerning patterns and practices by major type of service.
The fifth chapter takes up the question of organizing for
public service and examines organizational issues of
structure, policy, reward systems, and resources. A con-

---

[1]While service to the federal government could have been included as an
important form of college and university public service, it has not been included because the issues and practices are so complex, changeable, and
intertwined with the research mission in higher education. Adequate treatment of this subject requires a separate monograph.

cluding section comments on the major issues surrounding public service and recommends some areas for further research. Both are intended to be helpful to institutions and individuals interested in expanding and/or modifying their public service mission and activities or in further studying public service in higher education.

SERVICE AS A MISSION:
Alternative Concepts and Perspectives

Is service an important or even an appropriate mission for higher education? Should it stand alongside research and teaching as an equally important mission or be relegated to a distant third as so many presently claim? How should service activities be related to teaching and research programs? What kinds of activities should be labeled service? Among the many possible groups with whom it is possible to form service relationships—the community; local, state, and federal government; business and industry—which are the most deserving of our attention? Should we formulate priorities? Who decides about service? The purpose of this chapter is to review current concepts of service and their historical precedents to better understand how some have answered or approached these questions.

We are a long way from a theory of service whether we use theory in the formal sense of theory as explanation, or theory as conceptual framework, or even theory as ideology or general consensus about what we should do. Discussions of service in the literature do not involve theorizing in any "pure" sense. Rather, they involve an ongoing debate centered in rival positions concerning the role of service in higher education—positions so disparate that on one end of the spectrum are those who see service as the raison d'être of higher education and on the other are those who would reject it altogether as inappropriate or even inimical to the enterprise. In part this disparity results from the confusions of definition. But it is more than a definitional problem. The differences over service also result from differing views about higher education as a whole—its purposes, priorities, and relationships to the social, political, and economic order. The most profound insights on service are found in the discussions of the philosophy and purposes of higher education and, most directly, in the debates over the relationship between higher education and society.

The history of higher education in the United States is a history of the development of institutions and of educational patterns and practices in the context of an evolving economic, political, and social environment. Colleges and universities have always depended on the larger society for their clientele and economic support and have used a concept of service to describe their activities in relation to that larger society. Service provides the rationale for societal involvement with and support of higher education.

Service provides the rationale for societal involvement with and support of higher education

---

Service also provides a justification for change and academic reform. Throughout our history, arguments for changes in curriculum and clientele, in programs and activities, and in structure and organization have been buttressed by the claim that the change would allow higher education to serve society better. Service is nearly always emphasized.

With the land grant movement and the development of universities in the late 1800s, service came to mean much more. It came to mean a specific mission and a variety of activities planned and executed on behalf of some special group or constituency external to the campus. The service orientation of colleges and universities began to be described as uniquely American and one of the great strengths of American higher education.

For all of this use of the term, however, public service remains a fuzzy and difficult concept. This chapter examines three popular metaphors of higher education—ivory tower, social service station, and culture mart—that accentuate rival conceptions of higher education and quite different perspectives on service. It also reviews four differing propositions concerning the role of service in higher education and how it is best fulfilled—through ideas of value, through social problem solving, through social criticism, and through social activism. While these alternative conceptions and propositions are synthesized from the current literature on higher education, they reflect a rich history of constant adaptation and evolution of the idea and the ideal of service. The last section of this chapter traces that history in broad strokes.

Metaphors and Perspectives on Higher Education and Service
The metaphor of the ivory tower is popular and persistent. Described but not advocated by Henderson (1968) and Wolff (1969), it depicts colleges and universities as isolated and autonomous enclaves of scholars and students intentionally separated from the ongoing activities and controversies of the "real world." The institution becomes a sanctuary, protected by clearly established boundaries between the institution and the rest of society (Wolff 1969).

The work of the ivory tower is to preserve and pass on the cultural heritage and to pursue truth through objective and disinterested scholarship. Enduring values are taught along with the skills of critical thinking and analysis. The important questions of the day—"real world" problems—are examined through discourse, research, and scholarship. Students are prepared to grapple with these problems as active and involved citizens.

In this perspective of higher education, the ivory tower's service to society lies precisely in its educational and research functions, in its preservation and transmission of the cultural heritage, and in its pursuit of truth. Education is service; the pursuit of truth is service. The boundaries between the institution and society should be maintained so that the institution can fulfill these important functions.

Ivory towers also serve by making it possible for faculty members and students to engage in social criticism, to point out failures and faults in the existing political, social, and economic order, and to suggest remedies and alternatives.

> *The Wisconsin idea . . . bartered the German concept that the faculty of a university should remain independent and objective critics of the state for a new concept that they should be regarded as employed servants of the state. . . . It is only recently that American universities have been faced with the costs of the barter: a servant cannot be an independent and objective critic, and just now the nation needs criticism from its faculty members more than it needs service. If the boundaries which contain, and to some degree isolate, the university dissolve, the university will do less well its unique job for society* (Ashby 1971, p. 106).

Social criticism becomes a form of service and a justification for the existence and preservation of colleges and universities as ivory towers.

While the image of higher education as social service station dates to Veblen in the early 1900s (1957) and Flexner (1930), they used the metaphor disparagingly. It is usually associated with Clark Kerr's image of the multiversity and his discussion of the uses of the university (1972). Kerr is often depicted as the "philosopher" and "apologist" for this vision of higher education (Adelman 1973; Wolff 1969), though Kerr himself insists that his work is descriptive rather than prescriptive (1972, p. 146).

In any case, the essence of the college or university as social service station is the social importance of knowledge.

Knowledge is now central to society. It is wanted, even demanded, by more people and more institutions than ever before. The university as producer, wholesaler, and retailer of knowledge cannot escape service. Knowledge today is for everybody's sake (Kerr 1972, p. 114).

The service of higher education is to produce and provide knowledge to students and to other social institutions. The boundaries between institutions of higher education and society become ever more porous as knowledge expands and as the university responds to ever-increasing demands from more and various external groups.

Kerr provides an enduring picture of the multiversity as social service station in his description of the University of California in the 1960s:

The University of California last year [1962] had . . . operations in over a hundred locations, counting campuses, experiment stations, agricultural and urban extension centers, and projects abroad involving more than fifty countries; . . . [and] some form of contact with nearly every industry, nearly every level of government, nearly every person in its region. . . . It will soon also have 100,000 students—30,000 of them at the graduate level—yet much less than one-third of its expenditures are directly related to teaching. It already has nearly 200,000 students in extension courses—including one out of every three lawyers and one out of every six doctors in the state (Kerr 1972, pp. 7–8).

The metaphor of social service station seems irresistible to philosophers of higher education and often becomes the point of departure for differing visions of higher education. Unfortunately, in the process the image also becomes fuzzy. Adelman, a Canadian commentator on higher education, argues that since the late 1800s, the social service station model has been the dominant model for higher education in the United States (1973). His description of the model emphasizes the "massification" of higher education (the tremendous increase in the number of people taking advantage of higher education), higher education as a means of upward mobility, and the socialization for all types of work through vocational training, as well as direct services for external groups. He stresses that while the social service station is avowedly neutral, it in fact accepts the dominant values of the surrounding society.

Wolff (1969) also picks up on the image of social service station but sees it as a "projection of present trends and . . . a prediction of the shape of the university to come" (p. 3). In his critique of Kerr's *Uses of the University,* he criticizes Kerr for the "failure to draw a sharp distinction between the concepts of effective or market demand and human or social need" (p. 36), quoting as evidence a number of Kerr's references to national and social needs. Wolff argues that "a human or social need is a want, a lack, the absence of something material or social . . . [and further that] societies of men have collective needs, for social justice, for peace, for cultural and political community" (p. 37). Demand or market demand, on the other hand, refers to the existence in a market economy of buyers with money in hand who are prepared to spend it for a particular commodity. The failure to distinguish between demands and social or national needs leads to "a covert ideological rationalization for whatever human or social desires happen to be backed by enough money or power to translate them into effective demands" (p. 39). Wolff argues that Kerr is guilty of this covert rationalization and uses as example Kerr's description of the federal grant university as an instrument of national purpose. The extensive war and defense–related research activities of universities, then, are responses to national needs that Kerr seemingly endorses. Wolff concludes by asking:

> *At the present time in the United States, is there a greater social need for full scale integration of the resources and activities of the universities into existing domestic and foreign programs, or for a sustained critique of those programs from an independent position of authority and influence?* (p. 42).

He favors the role of social criticism and therefore rejects the multiversity and the social service station. The failure to distinguish between market demands and social and national needs pervades the literature on service; hence, Wolff's criticism of Kerr could be applied with equal force and validity to many subsequent discussions of service.

Adelman (1973) proposed the metaphor of the culture mart; it represents the future direction of higher education. In this view, the already porous boundaries between institutions of higher education and other societal institutions are totally demolished. Educational activities occur in all types of institutions and throughout individuals' life spans. The role of colleges and universities as institutions is to serve as brokers, validating and legitimizing educational activities of all types wherever they occur. They are quintessentially service institutions. This view of higher education is particularly evident in much of the literature about community colleges (Cohen and Brawer 1982; Gleazer 1980; Gollattscheck et al. 1976). Interestingly, we have returned to a definition of service as education and education as service similar to that of the ivory tower but from a radically different perspective or conception of higher education.

Rival Perspectives on Forms of Service

Four different propositions concerning how the service role in higher education is best fulfilled—service through ideas of value, service through social criticism, service through social problem solving, and service through social activism—are also evident in the literature on higher education and on service. While they do not follow directly from the various metaphors and conceptions of higher education and the service mission, they do provide further elaboration of alternative ideas concerning how to serve.

In a rare sustained discussion of the service mission in higher education, Martin (1977) argues that the nature of the educational enterprise is to be of service to society. He redefines research and teaching as forms of service. According to Martin, the most important service of higher education is to help the individual to develop "ideas of value" and to cope with contending ideas of value—individualism and communitarianism, quality and quantity (1977), science and humanities, faith and reason (1982).

It is this grappling with issues of value—this determination to not simply reflect the tensions existing in society but instead to somehow provide useful responses to them—that makes college and university teaching and research essential services to the nation. This task, in which ideas of importance are dealt with, criticized, refined, reordered, and brought to the attention of individuals and other institutions, is perhaps the core service of higher education (1977, p. 13).

Martin also argues that the best rationale for the university is that it is a place where the most substantial issues of society—political, economic, and social—receive sustained and disciplined attention and that it is the place where prospects are best for the emergence of appropriate responses (1982).

Others argue that the most important form of service is social criticism (Ashby 1971; Dressel and Faricy 1972; Henderson 1968; Wolff 1969). As noted earlier, social criticism is a primary justification for the preservation of distinct boundaries between colleges and universities and the surrounding society.

Social criticism is the most important service of the college or university, primarily because educational institutions are currently the only institutions providing sustained criticism capable of leading to the renewal of society. The church is dismissed as having chosen to ignore the role, the media for being too superficial (Bok 1982). Traditions of autonomy and academic freedom buttress the role of social criticism and are in turn buttressed by it. During the late 1960s and early 1970s, much concern was expressed over the politicalization of the university, and commentators rushed to assert that the independence so essential to academic freedom and social criticism for faculty and students could be preserved only if institutions as institutions refrained from taking stands on political and other issues (Ashby 1971; Minter and Thompson 1968). This position continues to be supported (Bok 1982) and to be criticized by activists who argue that the failure to take stands is in effect a political position in defense of the status quo (Luria and Luria 1970; Wofford 1968).

Service through social problem solving seems to be the most popular conception of the best form of service (Kerr 1972). In this view, faculty and students in the disciplines and the professions actively concern themselves with ways in which knowledge can be applied to the solution of contemporary social problems. Students engage in real-world problem solving through internships and practical experiences, even though the primary thrust of the academic program remains that of preparing students for future roles as professionals and concerned citizens. Faculty become involved in social problem solving through consultation and other activities, although they must take care not to allow such activities to jeopardize their primary responsibilities to teaching and research. Colleges and universities as institutions join with governments at all levels, with communities, and with various other external groups in efforts to apply scientific and technical knowledge to complex social problems. In this way, institutions apply a publicly provided reservoir of skills to improving the quality of life.

One argument in favor of service through social problem solving is that colleges and universities should involve themselves in real problems to remain vital teaching and research institutions. Service is thus "good" for the institution (Kerr 1972; Wofford 1968). Another argument is that social problem solving is consistent with the social responsibilities of higher education.

> *That the university has an obligation for public service is no longer in question. The points at issue are the ways in which it is appropriate for the university to serve society* (Henderson 1968, p. 1).

The Carnegie Foundation for the Advancement of Teaching (1967) endorsed the concept and mission of service in the context of social problem solving and offered as a "precept" that colleges and universities should participate in public service activities that are a direct outgrowth of regular teaching and research programs and that in turn feed back and strengthen them.

Bok (1982) comes to much the same conclusion but introduces some cautionary notes:

> *Universities have an important responsibility to address social needs through their normal academic functions, such as teaching programs, research, or technical assistance. . . . In contrast, however, it is much harder to justify the use of nonacademic methods such as divesting*

stock, boycotting suppliers, or issuing formal institu-
tional statements on political issues. . . . Universities
have an obligation to serve society by making the contri-
butions they are uniquely able to provide. [At the same
time, however, they must protect equally important
interests of] the preservation of academic freedom, the
maintenance of high intellectual standards, the protec-
tion of academic pursuits from outside interference, the
rights of individuals affected by the university not to be
harmed in their legitimate interests (p. 88).

Babbidge (1968) states a similar theme somewhat differently:

Colleges and universities have been urged to enlist in
armies doing battle with everything from poverty to
underdevelopment. Academic troops are being deployed
against cancer, stroke, and heart disease. . . . There can
be no doubt . . . that the uses of the university to which
President Kerr alluded have pronounced appeal for a
socially minded, activist administration. And there can be
no doubt, either, that college presidents are worried
about the effects of such use upon their institutions. They
know their colleges and universities are not universal
joints, capable of turning in all directions. Nor are they
bottomless pools of intellectual resource. They don't
want to be unpatriotic or socially unresponsive, but
college presidents increasingly wonder how many such
projects they can take on and how much they can afford
to contribute. . . . Some [college presidents] feel they are
being ravaged in the name of public service. All are
conscious of being pulled and tugged at (pp. 325–26).

Some, however, criticize the adoption of this approach to
service. Lowi (1970), in his political analysis of higher
education, argues that if it adopts the problem-solving
approach, which he equates with a technocratic education
model, higher education ends up providing service to a
regime, and the relationship is master-servant. Lowi is
primarily interested in an analysis of the relationship of
educational systems and class interests. He describes two
fundamentally different types of service, which he thinks
are often confused in the literature. The older concept of

service in a functional or sociological sense implies that "there is a section of society in which a certain kind of educational output can find a grounding" (p. 247). In the history of higher education in the United States, classical education "served" the aristocracy in this sense as liberal arts colleges served the bourgeoisie. Disciplinary education, the fusion of teaching and research, and graduate and professional education "served" the middle classes, while practical and vocational education "served" the working classes. Lowi argues that service in this sense does not involve a causal relationship. Rather, it involves a "provider/demander" relationship (p. 243) with the clientele providing the social base necessary to ensure that the institution prospers. The newer concept of service, according to Lowi, views technocratic systems of education as responsible for solving the social and economic problems of the surrounding society and creates a causal relationship of the master-servant type. Colleges and universities become servants to the regime and must provide whatever services are demanded of them or suffer direct consequences in the loss of essential resource support. Lowi finds it bitterly ironic that the shift to the master-servant relationship had its impetus from inside rather than outside colleges and universities, that is, from the desire of faculty members and students and finally institutions themselves to engage in social problem solving. Others do not go as far as Lowi in their criticism of the problem-solving approach, but they wonder whose purposes are being served (Luria and Luria 1970).

The approach of service through social activism goes beyond service through social problem solving and involves faculty and students and even institutions themselves as direct participants in real-world controversies.[2] The impetus for this approach came from the student and faculty critiques of higher education during the late 1960s. Many argued that colleges and universities, but particularly multiversities, were deeply enmeshed in complicitous action in full partnership with a military-industrial complex that they considered repressive and unjust. What was needed, according to this view, was social activism of behalf

[2]See Lowi (1970) and Bok (1982) for descriptions of the social activist view.

of better causes—social justice, humanitarianism, equal opportunity and antidiscrimination, environmental protection, and so on (Johnson 1968). Colleges and universities, not only in their teaching, research, and service but also as institutions wielding considerable political influence in society, had an obligation, according to this view, to become more socially active institutions.

Wofford (1968) argued forcefully for this position in the late 1960s, asserting that the university is by its nature an agent of politics and change. Colleges and universities too often respond to external pressures instead of addressing internally the difficult questions about truth and justice.

> *I am afraid that . . . we will respond to these [external] pressures as we have with other forms of public service that our universities render. We will give public service in the service-station sense. We give governors and farmers and embalming associations the service they ask for— which is not necessarily the service which they and our society need. And we do it as something above and beyond what we see as our true academic duty. We do it as an extra favor and for good profit. We do it in performance of that third competing obligation of a university.*
> *I am skeptical of competing purposes and especially third purposes* (Wofford 1968, p. 20).

. . . the university has an obligation . . . to address the difficult public questions of the day . . .

Wofford argued instead that the first and primary purpose of a university is seeking truth and if that purpose leads the university into social and/or political action, so be it. Even though the consequences are not always easy to take, the university has an obligation as an institution to address the difficult public questions of the day—war, peace, and social justice.

The debate over service through social activism led, however, to concern about the politicization of higher education and to fear for the preservation of academic freedom and of institutional independence. Many argued that higher education had gone too far and should retreat to a less active role in society.

We have, then, many different conceptions, perspectives, and propositions on the mission, role, and best form of service for higher education. Bok (1982) articulates perhaps most clearly the dominant view. Colleges and universities have social responsibilities, but they fulfill them through social problem-solving activities that are closely connected with their teaching and research functions and through a variety of technical assistance programs and other direct service activities. Institutions refrain from many forms of social activism to protect the rights and freedoms of faculty members and students and to safeguard the independence of colleges and universities from other of society's institutions. While colleges and universities, particularly public institutions, should be responsive to social needs where appropriate and feasible, institutions must maintain the right to decide for themselves, through normal mechanisms of governance, which forms of service and which particular activities are appropriate.

Evolution of the Idea and Ideal of Service
The concept of service in higher education was first used in a general sense to justify societal support of higher education and was closely related to educational mission (Rudolph 1962).[3] The education of students for particular roles and responsibilities was said to be a service to society. Colonial colleges "served" society by educating the religious leaders for communities dominated by religious influences (Rudolph 1962). As colonies, later states, grew into more complex social organizations, colleges served by educating political, social, and professional elites (Everett 1848; Rudolph 1962). In a democratic republic, the education of the voting citizen becomes the college's service to democracy (Brubacher and Rudy 1976; Nevins 1962). As the industrial and economic base of American society becomes more complex and dependent upon technological and scientific advances, colleges and universities serve by providing specialized and professional education and training (Draper 1907). This use of the concept of service, adapted to the current situation, is obviously still with us in the metaphor of the ivory tower and the proposition for service through ideas of value.

A related use of the concept of service in connection with the research mission appears with the development of

[3]It is obviously impossible to review the entire literature on the history of higher education in the United States to review the evolution of the concept of service. Therefore, three well-known works were used as a starting point (Hofstader and Smith 1961; Rudolph 1962; Veysey 1965), and other sources were consulted on the basis of the material in those works.

universities in the late 1800s and early 1900s. Universities serve society—and deserve support in return—by producing the knowledge essential to industrial, technological, and even political social advances (Veysey 1965). This concept of service, adapted to a current context, is also still with us and related most directly to the image of social service station.

Through the history of American higher education, the concept of service has also been used to provide a rationale and justification for curricular and programmatic change or for the initiation of new programs and activities in higher education (Eddy 1957; Nevins 1962; Rudolph 1962; Veysey 1965). The use of the service idea first became evident in the reaction against the classical curriculum of the colonial period and early 1800s. Benjamin Franklin and later Thomas Jefferson argued that American society needed a more practical curriculum, one better suited to growth and expansion (Rudolph 1962; Veysey 1965). Many argued for more scientific courses in the curriculum. Affiliated scientific schools in several colleges were developed—finally and after some resistance—as a service to society (Rudolph 1962). Veysey (1965) notes, however, that "before the Civil War . . . spokesmen for this point have usually been found outside the academic establishment rather than within it" (pp. 59–60).

After the Civil War, the idea of service became more clearly articulated as a mission for higher education and more clearly associated with special kinds of programs and activities. Veysey (1965) traced the emergence of the American university from 1865 through 1915 by tracing three specific concepts of higher education (rather than the vague word university) and by tracing their related institutional forms and practices.

These [concepts] centered, respectively, in the aim of practical public service, in the goal of abstract research on what was believed to be the pure German model, and finally in the attempt to diffuse standards of cultivated taste (p. 12).

Each of these concepts fought for a place and ascendancy in the order of things. The aim of practical public service, according to Veysey, was considered "the genuinely American contribution to educational theory" (p. 12), but he traced utilitarian enthusiasm at least to Francis Bacon.[4] The advocates of public service, however, include a host of distinguished university presidents—Eliot of Harvard (1869; Hofstader and Smith 1961), White of Cornell (Veysey 1965), Gilman of California (1872), Angell of Michigan (Veysey 1965), James (1905) and Draper (1907) of Illinois, Van Hise of Wisconsin (1910; Brubacher and Rudy 1976), and Wilson of Princeton (Hofstader and Smith 1961).

While the idea of colleges' and universities' providing direct or special services to the larger society is not unique, American colleges and universities realized this ideal in specific institutional forms, programs, and activities to an extent that is unparalleled elsewhere.

The most celebrated and successful example of the articulation and fulfillment of the service ideal is the land grant college (Eddy 1957; Geiger 1963; Kerr 1961; Nevins 1962). The Morrill Act of 1862 provided federal funds to state governments for the purpose of supporting a special kind of institution that was responsive "to the needs of a practical, growing people . . . [and] to industrial and agricultural progress" (Nevins 1962, p. 11). The Morrill Act dictated curriculum (study of agriculture and the mechanic arts) and to a certain extent clientele (the agricultural and working classes) but left all other matters to state governments and to the institutions themselves.

The land grant idea gradually evolved and assumed a number of different service orientations. "The most important idea in the genesis of the land grant colleges and state universities was that of democracy" (Nevins 1962, p. 16), referring to service to an open, mobile society in which opportunity exists and in which the political system remains free and responsive to the wishes of an educated citizenry. Colleges and universities became essential to such a society. As Andrew Draper, president of the University of Illinois and later with the Department of Education, noted in 1907:

[4]Veysey uses the word "utility" more often than service, arguing that service loses clarity because it is used both too broadly and too narrowly (footnote, p. 60). By utility, however, he usually means public service.

*We will build up institutions which make for scholarship,
for freedom and for character, and which, withal, will
look through American eyes upon questions of political
policy, and train American hands to deftness in the
constructive and manufacturing industries of most
concern to the United States* (p. 38).

Experimentation and extension were also associated with
the land grant idea. The Hatch Act of 1887 provided additional funds for experiment stations at the land grant
colleges in which the agricultural problems actually encoun-
tered within the state could be addressed. Extension
programs and services were made possible by funds provided as a result of the Smith Lever Act of 1914. Their
purpose was to disseminate the results of agricultural
research throughout a state.

By 1914, most of the original land grant colleges had
evolved into state universities and had taken on a variety of
other service responsibilities (Eddy 1957; Nevins 1962). The
land grant model, however, provides a powerful and lasting
model for public service, and a variety of relatively recent
attempts have been made to replicate it in other areas like
education, public health, and urban services. Before
examining them, however, it is necessary to trace the ideal
of service in its other manifestations during the period of the
emergence of the university.

The presidents of two major private universities, White of
Cornell[5] and Eliot of Harvard, regarded themselves "as
showing the way to the service-oriented university in
America" during the later part of the nineteenth century
(Veysey 1965, p. 81). White contributed the notions of
institutional commitment to religious freedom and to
freedom of choice in a curriculum in which all subjects were
considered to be of equal value (Veysey 1965). He also
described the university as a "training ground for politically
oriented public service" (Veysey 1965, p. 85). Eliot (1869)
contributed the elective system and the belief in the value

[5]Cornell is the land grant institution in New York, but it differs from most
land grant institutions because it is a private university. It was founded and
given generous support by Ezra Cornell in 1868, and its development as a
university therefore provides an excellent opportunity to examine a new
conception of the American university.

and utility of professional education (Hofstader and Smith 1961; Veysey 1965).

The mission of service became most fully realized, however, in the state universities of the West. Gilman, in his 1872 inaugural address as president of the newly founded University of California, called for a modern curriculum, including sciences, undergraduate and graduate programs, and professional preparation. More importantly, he emphasized the orientation to the state:

> . . .*The charter and the name declare that this is the University of . . . this State. It must be adapted to this people, to their public and private schools, to their peculiar geographical position, to the requirements of their new society and their undeveloped resources* (1872, p. 157).

State universities in the West differed from other and earlier colleges and universities in their commitment to state service. What became known as the "Wisconsin Idea" "did not exist only in Wisconsin" (Veysey 1965, p. 73), but it was most pronounced there. Lincoln Steffens, discussing the University of Wisconsin in 1909, said:

> *What the brain is to a man's hands, feet and eyes, this university is to the people of the state: the instinctive resource for information, light and guidance. And the state itself . . . draws constantly upon the faculty* (1909, p. 132).

The Wisconsin Idea equaled the land grant college as a powerful model of public service for higher education. Its early advocates included Charles K. Adams of Michigan (Brubacher and Rudy 1976; Veysey 1965), William Watts Folwell of Minnesota (Brubacher and Rudy 1976; Veysey 1965), and Frederick Jackson Turner (Veysey 1965). Nevins (1962) thinks, however, that Charles Van Hise, president of the University of Wisconsin from 1904 until 1918, was the most persuasive spokesman of the service mission in higher education. According to Van Hise, "The university would be a watchtower, taking an active part in improving society, serving as an essential instrument of public service" (Brubacher and Rudy 1976, p. 166). The boundaries of the university would be coterminous with those of the state, and the primary purpose of the university would be to service the needs of the state and its citizens.

The two most important means of such service, beyond the agricultural base provided by land grant institutions, were university extension and a direct relationship with state government (Brubacher and Rudy 1976). The extension service of the land grant model disseminated the results of research and experimentation. Van Hise used the idea of extension service and developed courses on all kinds of subjects, which were made available throughout the state to people from all walks of life. "By 1910, over 5,000 people were taking the university's correspondence courses" (Brubacher and Rudy 1976, p. 166). He also developed direct services for state and local government.

Robert LaFollette, named governor of Wisconsin in 1901, "first formed a braintrust of expert advisers and administrators drawn from the University campus" (Geiger 1963, pp. 68–69). By 1910:

A Bureau of General Welfare answered thousands of factual questions about sanitation, economics, sociology, government, and education. University shops and laboratories tested soils, ores, fuels, clays, and water. A Bureau of Debating and Public Discussion sponsored debates throughout the state on controversial issues and loaned package libraries of selected materials to local discussion groups. The university thus was becoming one with the state; its campus in truth was the whole state of Wisconsin (Brubacher and Rudy 1976, p. 166).

During the same period, other types of institutions became concerned with national service. In 1896, Woodrow Wilson, then president of Princeton, eloquently made the case for the mission of national service and its related educational implications:

Of course, when all is said, it is not learning but the spirit of service that will give a college place in the public annals of the nation. It is indispensable, it seems to me, if it is to do its right service, that the air of affairs should be admitted to all its class-rooms. I do not mean the air of party politics, but the air of the world's transactions, the consciousness of the solidarity of the race, the sense of the duty of man toward man, of the presence of men in every problem, of the significance of truth for guidance as well as for knowledge, of the potency of ideas, of the promise and the hope that shine in the face of all knowledge. There is laid upon us the compulsion of the national life. We dare not keep aloof and closet ourselves while a nation comes to its maturity (1896, p. 694).

Municipal service was an equally potent ideal. The types of institutions with a mission of service to urban areas established during the late 1800s varied greatly (Brubacher and Rudy 1976; Kolbe 1928) as did the forms of support for such institutions. The American municipal university helped provide for educational opportunity and curricular diversity and helped "meet the sweeping public demand . . . for more direct service to a fast-industrializing and urbanizing society" (Brubacher and Rudy 1976, p. 170). The characteristics of an urban university were:

1. "Departure from the traditional curriculum to include fields of knowledge useful to the urban community";
2. Equal opportunity;
3. Public support;
4. "Encouragement of private gifts, particularly for purposes specifically useful to the community";
5. "Cooperation of science with industry and all other useful manifestations of urban life";
6. Education of adults (Kolbe 1928, p. 50).

In the early 1900s, universities—public and private, rural and municipal—began to develop and expand professional schools in response to demands for more extensive and coherent preparation for all types of professional practice and employment. Professional schools in turn developed extensive direct service relationships with external groups (Rudolph 1962).

The increasingly important mission of public service and its ever-expanding role and function in higher education were not universally accepted in higher education, however. Thorstein Veblen, writing in the early 1900s, wanted to ban professional and technological schools from the campus because universities should be concerned with the search for pure knowledge; he wanted little or no contact with the external world (1957). Robert Hutchins (1936) thought universities were losing sight of their main aim because of "love of money." He too opposed research intended to solve the practical problems of the day. Abraham Flexner asked in 1930:

> *Why do certain American universities feel themselves under pressure to develop their "service" functions, even to call themselves "public service" institutions? There are many reasons. State universities have to make themselves "useful"—or they think they do—in order to justify themselves to the man in the street or on the farm. since income depends on appropriations of the state legislature; thus large numbers—some resident, others non-resident—get the kind of information or training, which they need or think they need, and from which they feel themselves competent to profit—though, as I have urged and shall continue to urge, this sort of thing does not deserve to be called college or university education at all; endowed institutions think they must be useful in order that alumni, local communities, and the general public may be encouraged to contribute gifts, and in order that they may not be reproached for being aristo-cratic or "high-brow" or careless of the needs of the general public. And when I say "useful," I mean directly, immediately useful, for Americans like to see "results." I believe that the intelligence and generosity of the Ameri-can public—including alumni—are thus underestimated and undermined (1930, p. 914).*

Despite the dissenting voices, however, the number of professional programs expanded dramatically, colleges and universities gradually assumed more and more direct service activities on behalf of federal, state, or local govern-ment or some more specialized interest group, and faculty members and students became more numerous and more active. Universities begin to look like the multiversities Kerr described (1972) and begin to be defined in positive terms as social service stations. Community colleges were established with the specific mission of providing service to communities. Although it is the object of many different conceptions and attitudes, public service has assumed an important and distinctive place in American higher education.

COMMUNITY SERVICE

Most college and university public service is community service in that it consists of activities involving individuals and communities within the immediate vicinity of the campus. Communities can be urban or rural, large or small, heterogeneous or homogeneous, affluent or impoverished. Colleges and universities of all types, sizes, and forms of control engage in community services according to their distinctive interpretations of their missions, roles, and responsibilities, their academic programs and resources, and the interests of faculty and students. While all types of institutions are engaged in community service, for some the activity is distinctly peripheral to their more fundamental missions of teaching and research. For others, community service is more central. The community college has most fully embraced the mission of public service and has assimilated community service as part of its institutional identity and value system (Myran 1978a).

Community groups served by colleges and universities include various civic, neighborhood, and professional groups and service agencies, municipal, county, or state government agencies, and local businesses and industries. Relationships and types of services vary not only by college or university provider but also by the needs and characteristics of the community group or agency being served and by the type of community.

In this section, the general issues, controversies, patterns, and practices of community service provided by all types of colleges and universities are discussed, first for community colleges and then more broadly for urban areas.

Community Service by Community Colleges

Many consider a strong commitment to the community the very essence of the community college—what makes it distinctly different from other types of colleges and universities.

The community college has a responsibility to function as an integral part of the fabric and rhythm of the communities it serves, and it should make a significant and positive difference in the quality of life in those communities (Myran 1974, pp. 1–2).

The commitment itself is often defined as service. The service of the community college is often taken to mean access—finding a place for community residents, young and old, from all racial and ethnic backgrounds, including the educationally disadvantaged (Carnegie Commission 1970). Service might be provided through a diverse array of educational programs—college transfer, terminal career preparation, and personal enrichment. An increasingly popular view, best voiced by Harlacher, stresses community-based education that emphasizes the community's involvement in the educational process as well as access and lifelong education (Yarrington 1974). Thus, the distinctions between direct service activities, educational programs, and clientele are blurred, and the concept of community service becomes intertwined with notions of continuing education, lifelong learning, and community-based education.

This section traces the history of service in the community college and examines four conceptually distinct yet service-related activities in community colleges—community services, continuing education and lifelong learning, community-based education, and community renewal. For each, current practices are described and the scope of activity within community colleges delineated.

During their early years, two-year, junior colleges stressed the notion of college, a place for post–high school academic instruction. A special orientation toward the community, however, begins to appear in the literature as early as the 1920s. Koos (1925) suggested that junior colleges offer courses adapted to local needs. The American Association of Junior Colleges (now the American Association of Community and Junior Colleges—AACJC) added the following to its definition of the junior college in 1925:

> The junior college may, and is likely to, develop a different type of curriculum suited to the larger and ever changing civic, social, religious, and vocational needs of the entire community in which the college is located (Bogue 1950, p. 17).

In 1931, Eells defined junior college service as meeting "community needs as distinguished from those of the youth who compose its regular student body" (p. 235). In 1936, Hollinshead wrote that the junior college should be concerned with recreational, vocational, and cultural activities and with adult education.

The community college has most fully embraced the mission of public service . . .

Cohen and Brawer (1982) note that every book written about community colleges since Hollinshead's work in 1936 has stressed the community orientation and commitment of the community college (p. 15). Of particular influence was *The Community College,* written in 1950 by Jesse Bogue, then executive secretary of the American Association of Junior Colleges. Bogue argued for a strong commitment to the community and for adult education in the community college.

During their early years, junior colleges stressed academic transfer programs and articulation with four-year institutions. At the same time, however, private junior colleges, and later public two-year colleges, claimed as service the fact that they were cultural and recreational centers for their communities. Such community service was recognized as particularly important in rural areas without other access to cultural events and recreational facilities. In some areas, such service remains an important community service of the community college.

In the 1960s, junior and community colleges began to develop, often in collaboration with local employers, specific career preparation programs. The number and size of such programs grew rapidly over the years, so rapidly that today career programs represent the dominant component of the community college curriculum. Career preparation programs were heralded as a service to local businesses and industries looking for trained and educated personnel and as a service to local residents seeking employment or opportunities for career advancement. Whether defined as education or service, the phenomenal growth of such programs and of the community college sector as a whole suggests that they were clearly responsive to community needs. (Such programs also contributed, of course, to the public perception of higher education as preparation for specific jobs—a perception that many have begun to see as detrimental to higher education.)

The Carnegie Commission on Higher Education (1970) advocated the expansion of the community college sector in higher education because it saw community colleges as essential to the achievement of two important social goals—access and equal opportunity. According to the commission, community colleges had inherited the concept of service from land grant institutions and reshaped it to meet community needs through academic transfer, occupational and general education programs, *and* direct services.

By the 1970s, then, community service was clearly recognized as an essential activity of the community college. Service was defined, however, to include curriculum and clientele as well as cultural and recreational programs. This extremely broad conception of service continued throughout the 1970s as concepts of continuing education and adult education. Lifelong learning, community-based education, and community renewal were introduced, each stressing different combinations of academic program, clientele, and "other" activities. The literature on community colleges is primarily normative and polemical rather than analytical (with some exceptions, primarily Cohen [1969], Cohen and Associates [1975], Cohen and Brawer [1982]), making it difficult to categorize concepts and activity patterns. Very few empirical and/or large-scale descriptive studies provide a basis for identifying patterns and practices or for delineating the scope of community service activities. It is possible, however, to identify four distinct orientations to community service and to describe related activities—traditional community service, continuing education and related movements, community-based education, and community renewal.

The first might be labeled traditional community service—cultural, recreational, and other special programs aimed at the local community and its citizens. Most community colleges have an office of community services or a similar organizational unit that is responsible for the development of direct service programs. A wide variety of activities are organized, coordinated, monitored, or publicized by such offices: seminars, workshops, training programs, lectures, concerts, films, retreats, exhibitions, productions, publicity, science fairs, counseling, day care, leisure time programs, community development functions, credit and noncredit evening and off-campus courses, and the use of college facilities.

Nickens (1976) thinks of organized community services as a "delivery system" (pp. 12–13) for reaching out to the community and provides the taxonomy for community services shown in table 1. This conception and organization of community services has been supported by the National Council of Community Services (now the National Council

TABLE 1
TAXONOMY FOR COMMUNITY SERVICES

1.00 Instructional Services. Structured learning experiences designed to impart knowledge and develop skills, attitudes, insight, and values.

> **1.10 General Cultural Services.** Instructional activities designed to enhance a person's self-esteem, sense of well-being, and value to the community, family, and self.
>
> > **1.11 Community and Civic Affairs.**
> > - Educational programs will be provided for the elderly and disadvantaged to aid in their cultural, social, and economic development.
> > - Instruction will be given to help persons approaching retirement plan for this phase of their life.
> > - Programs will be offered to develop the citizenship skills of the poor, the unemployed, and the elderly.
> > - Communication skills will be improved, particularly the reading ability of members of disadvantaged groups.
> >
> > **1.12 Family Life.**
> > - Programs will be provided to help families understand and cope with alternate lifestyles in an effort to improve the quality of family life.
> > - Referral services and counseling will be provided for families experiencing alcohol or drug abuse.
> > - Day-care services will be provided for the children of parents attending evening or weekend programs.
> > - Programs will be provided to help low-income families with economic planning.
> > - Programs will be provided for developing meaningful, realistic, personal communication and healthy relationships within the family.
> > - Consumer education programs will be provided to improve the family economy.
> > - Instruction and counseling in family planning will be provided.
> > - Programs will be provided to assist the family in adjusting to major changes, such as birth, death, marriage, divorce, loss of job, and promotion.

1.13 Leisure-time and Recreational Activities.

- Various hobby skills will be taught to enrich leisure-time activities.
- Skills in sports and games will be taught to increase participation in recreational activities.
- Appropriate skills will be developed for effective membership and increased participation in clubs, organizations, and voluntary activities.
- Assistance will be provided for the attainment of wholesome, productive, and satisfying leisure-time activities for all community members.

1.14 Personal Health.

- Programs will be provided to help members of the community develop a more positive self-concept and an awareness of personal worth.
- Instruction in basic health maintenance will be provided for the disadvantaged members of the community.
- Programs will be provided to assist members of the community in coping with rapidly changing conditions in their environment.
- Instruction in home-nursing skills will be provided to members of the community.

1.15 Cultural Heritage and Enrichment.

- Cross-cultural programs will be provided to help promote understanding, tolerance, and appreciation of different cultures.
- Programs will be provided to help persons of different ethnic backgrounds acquire an appreciation of their cultural heritage.
- Programs will be provided to promote appreciation of the humanities.

1.20 Occupational Services. Instructional activities designed to create or improve the knowledge and skills required of persons in obtaining their livelihood.

1.21 Development of General Attitudes and Skills for a Career.

- Occupational information, testing, counseling, and referral services will be available for members of the community seeking employment.
- Academic counseling will be provided to persons desiring to develop a salable skill.
- Guidance and placement services will be

provided to persons desiring part-time jobs, especially retired persons, students, and housewives. Unemployed and underemployed persons will be taught how to write resumes, submit applications, and act on interviews.

- Communication will be maintained with employers to provide follow-up services and to evaluate the career program in the college.
- Remedial courses and developmental reading will be provided to increase educational and occupational effectiveness.
- The concept of career ladder will be developed based on input from the college, employers, and vocational educational centers, and implemented accordingly.
- Those whose jobs were discontinued will be given help in developing the necessary skills for reentering the job market.

1.22 Development of Specific Attitudes and Skills for a Career.

- Training and instruction will be provided in occupations most readily available in the community or nearby urban or industrial areas.
- Short courses and crash programs will be implemented to train persons when acute shortages exist in certain sectors of the job market.

2.00 Noninstructional Services. Coordination, consultation, or research and development undertaken in support of instructional services, program planning, and problem solving for individuals, groups, and agencies of the community.

2.10 Coordination. Services provided for the purpose of bringing agreement or compromise among persons, agencies, or a combination.

2.11 Individuals.

- Assistance will be provided to individuals in determining the proper agency for providing relief from a problem.
- Ombudsman services will be provided to individuals having difficulty acquiring aid from a particular agency.

2.12 Groups.

- The planning of community service projects will be coordinated with representatives of local clubs and organizations.

2.13 Agencies.
- The activities of all available agencies will be coordinated to give optimum assistance to community members.

2.20 Consultation. Professional or technical advice rendered by an individual or teams in areas of their expertise.

2.21 Consultation with Individuals.
- Guidance and technical expertise will be provided to individual teachers in the community as required to solve particular teaching problems.
- Technical advice will be available to persons involved in a study of community needs or problems.
- Consultation services will be provided to individuals having psychological, economic, or other personal problems; referrals will be made to appropriate agencies as necessary.

2.22 Consultation with Groups.
- Assistance will be provided to groups wishing to organize various activities in the community.
- The in-service education needs of employees of community industries and businesses will be identified.
- Strategies for teacher groups will be developed for improving teaching skills and methods.

2.23 Consultation with Agencies.
- Technical assistance will be provided to health agencies for alcohol and drug abuse educational programs.
- Assistance will be provided on the development of in-service programs for the staffs of hospitals, mental institutions, clinics, and nursing homes to improve care of patients.
- Assistance will be provided to agencies performing studies that will benefit the community.

2.30 Research and Development. Discovery and interpretation of information and relationships needed by the community to formulate plans for achieving desired outcomes.
- The present and future personnel needs of local businesses and industries will be assessed, the educational needs of specific groups identified, and appropriate strategies for meeting those needs developed.

3.00 Facility Services. The furnishing of real and material property, equipment, transportation, and energy required for community services.

- .The library, auditorium, classrooms, gymnasium, and athletic areas will be made available to members of the community when they are not required for college programs.
- A compromise will be formulated between conserving energy and providing services to the community.
- Bus routes and schedules will be implemented for members of the community using college facilities.
- Persons in the community will be allowed to use instructional, athletic, and other such devices and equipment when not required by college programs.

Source: John M. Nickens, *A Taxonomy for Community Services,* Reaching out through Community Services. New Directions for Community Colleges No. 14 (San Francisco: Jossey-Bass, 1976), pp. 11–12.

of Community Services and Continuing Education), founded in 1969 as an affiliate of the AACJC, and by the journal *Community Services Catalyst,* originally published in 1971. Both are intended to facilitate discussion of the service role in the community college. *Community Services Catalyst* also publishes useful descriptions of service activities.

Vaughan (1980), echoing Keim (1976) and Yarrington (1976), notes that despite the long history of emphasis on community services and despite the prominence given by AACJC leaders, community services are often "misunderstood and viewed as something of a stepchild" on community college campuses (p. 5). Yarrington argues that the mission and role of community services have not been clearly established and that the concept involves too many different ideas and directions.

A second yet related orientation to community service is represented by the continuing education, adult education, and lifelong learning movements in the community colleges. In many community colleges, continuing and adult education activities are grouped organizationally with community services into an office of community services and continuing education or some similar designation. Programs for adults have been defined as service since the 1930s and have been variously organized as continuing or adult education since that time. The most recent emphasis is on lifelong learning. The AACJC adopted as part of its mission statement in 1980 the organization of "national leadership and services for individual and community development through lifelong education" (Yarrington 1980, p. 8).

A great deal of attention has been devoted in the literature to defining—and defending—these concepts and their related activities (Cohen and Associates 1975; Harlacher 1969; Lombardi 1978; Myran 1969). Brawer (1980) has developed some useful composite definitions. Adult education is instruction

. . .designed to meet the unique needs of adults who are beyond the age of compulsory school attendance and who have either completed or interrupted their formal education. It may be provided by school systems, colleges, or other formal classes, correspondence study, radio, television, lectures, concerts, demonstrations, and counseling (Brawer 1980, p. 7).

Continuing education overlaps with adult education in its emphasis on adults, on multiple and nontraditional forms of delivery, and on the combination of credit, noncredit, or continuing education unit offerings, and in its provision by many different agencies and institutions. It carries, however, the implication of education for individuals "whose principal occupations are no longer as students, who seek learning as a means of developing one's potential or resolving personal, institutional, or community problems" (p. 8).

Lifelong learning overlaps with continuing education, essentially referring to "activities undertaken by adults who have left the traditionally sequenced educational system and who are interested in upgrading skills or in personal development" (p. 10). As with adult and continuing education, the delivery systems for lifelong learning vary, and multiple credit and noncredit modes are involved. Lifelong learning is usually equated with a philosophical position "that views the whole of society as a learning society . . ." (p. 10).

Often continuing education, adult education, and lifelong learning are lumped together as community education. The definition of community education that has gained the most widespread acceptance (Brawer 1980; Cohen and Brawer 1982) is one developed by Young, Fletcher, and Rue:

*[Community education includes] courses and activities
for credit or noncredit, formal classroom or nontraditional programs, [and] cultural, recreational offerings
specifically designed to meet the needs of the surrounding
community . . . [that use] school, college, or other
facilities. Programming is determined with input from the
community being served* (1978, p. 4).

It is extremely difficult to discern patterns in continuing
education, adult education, lifelong learning, and community education. The scope of the enterprise can be appreci-
ated to a certain extent through the examination of enrollment data for community education programs reported
annually for each state and institution in the AACJC *Community, Junior, and Technical College Directory.* Only
noncredit enrollments are included, however, and it should
be remembered that many institutions define continuing
education to include credit enrollments.

*Because degree credit courses are funded at a higher,
more consistent level than most of community education,
the tendency is to classify as much as possible as degree
credit, thus inflating those numbers at the expense of
community education enrollment figures* (Cohen and
Brawer 1982, p. 258).

In addition, AACJC cautions that because of variations in
program length and differing practices on registration and
collection, different institutions report enrollment figures
differently. The association reports, however, that noncredit enrollments grew from 3,259,972 in 1974–75 to 3,977,050
in 1979–80 to 4,088,513 in 1980–81, an increase between
1979–80 and 1980–81 of 2.8 percent. The total *credit* enrollment (head count) for the fall 1981 was 4,887,675, represent-
ing only a 1.27 percent increase over credit enrollments for
the previous year (pp. 18–19) and suggesting that community education represents a significant proportion of community college activity. The total community education
enrollment, however,

*. . . would far exceed the combined enrollment in the
career certificate and collegiate degree programs if
people enrolled in college credit classes but without*

degree aspirations were classified instead as adult basic education students, enrollees in short courses offered in continuing education programs, and participants in community service activities (Cohen and Brawer 1982, p. 258).

Young, Fletcher, and Rue (1978) conducted a survey on behalf of the AACJC Center for Community Education to investigate community services and community education at community colleges. They found strong support for the idea of community education from the 855 colleges responding to their survey. They listed 23 possible types of services and asked respondents if they were provided through "community services or the regular, continuing, or adult education programs of the colleges" (p. 5). Their results are shown in table 2. It is clear that community colleges are providing large numbers of community services.

A third strand in the literature on community service by community colleges focuses on community-based education. An outgrowth of community education, it is basically an attempt to emphasize community even more. Unlike community services or continuing education, there is usually no organizational unit in the community college responsible for community-based education because "community-based education . . . symbolizes an institutional value system; it is not a series of courses, an approach to instruction, or a description of the location of services or activities" (Myran 1978a, p. 1). The basic values represented by community-based education include the conviction that education can make a difference to all persons, that all have worth and potential, that education is a means of enriching lives and a recurring part of them. Community-based education requires a departure from total reliance on degree program offerings and a greater diversity of "programming, planning, organization, and delivery systems" (Myran 1978a, p. 5).

Community-based education has been emphasized in the writings of Cohen (1977), Cohen and Associates (1975), Gleazer (1974a, 1974b, 1980), Harlacher (1969), Myran (1974, 1978a), Yarrington (1980), and Young, Fletcher, and Rue (1978), all of whom have been leaders in the development of community colleges. In 1969, Cohen argued that community colleges should focus on community develop-

The basic values represented by community-based education include the conviction that education can make a difference to all persons . . .

TABLE 2
PROVISION OF COMMUNITY EDUCATION
OFFERINGS

Community Education Offering	Number of Colleges Providing Offering	Percent of 855 Community/ Junior Colleges Providing Offering
Guest lecturers or speakers bureau	587	68.6
College literary facilities	681	79.6
Help for business/industry to identify educational needs	680	79.5
Outreach counseling center	345	40.4
Public forums on local/state/ national problems	521	60.9
Assistance in planning conferences or workshops	671	78.5
Courses through television or other media	371	43.4
Orientation of college staff to community education	569	66.5
Dual enrollment and early admission program	613	71.7
Expertise in testing, reading, etc.	491	57.4
Cultural events	695	81.3
Computer/technical facilities	219	25.6

ment through active involvement in community planning and other activities that blend naturally into the learning activities of the college. Edmund Gleazer, president of the AACJC from 1958 to 1980, was a strong and influential advocate of community-based education. He asked: "What is it that people in the communities want and need to which the college can respond in service?" (1974a, p. 8); his response was to identify several kinds of community needs—career development, individual development, family development, and institutional development. "Needs and services may be as different as communities are different. A community college . . . will define its community and seek to develop its human resources" (1974a, p. 9).

Community-based education was given thrust as well through the establishment of COMBASE, a cooperative for the advancement of community-based postsecondary education. COMBASE provides an information center and

In-plant training programs for business/industry	610	71.3
Recreational facilities at no charge	492	57.5
Job placement services for adults	423	49.5
Credit outreach courses in prisons, etc.	428	50.0
Development of local performing arts group	411	48.1
Programs for minorities and other interest groups	653	76.4
Programs to upgrade job skills	755	88.3
Programs in consumer training	599	70.0
Adult basic education programs	573	67.0
Courses/services in health care	671	78.5
Programs in family life planning	504	58.9

Source: Robert B. Young, Suzanne M. Fletcher, and Robert R. Rue, "Directions for the Future: An Analysis of the Community Services Dimensions of Community Colleges" (Washington, D.C.: AACJC; and Ann Arbor: Office of Community Education Research, University of Michigan–Ann Arbor; 1978), p. 9.

a newsletter for the dissemination of information on community-based education programs.

Gilder and Rocha (1980) provide an interesting picture of the scope of community-based education. They report the results of a national survey conducted in 1978 by the Policies for Lifelong Education project of the AACJC. The purpose of the survey was to identify cooperative working relationships between community colleges and community groups. Only 173 colleges participated in the survey (about one-fifth of the respondents to the Young, Fletcher, and Rue survey of 1978), but those colleges identified more than 10,000 cooperative arrangements that served over 1.5 million people.

Gilder and Rocha divided their responses into ten major categories of cooperative agencies: local/state clubs and organizations, educational institutions, community groups, county governments, private enterprise, municipalities/local governments, occupational/vocational, federal government, state/regional governments, and unions (p. 12). They provided aggregate data on numbers of arrangements, numbers of persons served, and average number of persons served. Local/state clubs and organizations, educational institutions, community groups, and county governments enjoyed the largest number of cooperative arrangements with community colleges, although there were many collaborative arrangements with other groups as well. The detailed information on table 3 helps to suggest the range and scope of community services in the community college.

The table reveals that the collaboration of community colleges with other educational institutions, private enterprise, state government, and labor unions involved primarily credit and noncredit courses, while agreements with local clubs and organizations most often involved only the use of facilities. The funding base for the courses came from tuition and fees, while the colleges supported the costs of facilities for the collaborative arrangements with local clubs, organizations, and community groups.

The average college is a tangible resource to other community providers; their emerging mission as the nexus for learning seems solidly established by present activities and services (Gilder and Rocha 1980, p. 17).

A fourth and related strand in the literature on community colleges goes beyond community-based education to the concept of community renewal. It is perhaps the most radical and forward-looking notion of community service.

Alan Pifer, former president of the Carnegie Corporation of New York, was an early advocate of community renewal. He argued that community action is the basis for social reconstruction and that the community college should provide leadership for community action.

I'm going to make the outrageous suggestion that community colleges should start thinking about themselves from now on only secondarily as a sector of higher education and regard as their primary role community leadership (1974, p. 23).

Others also advocate the concept of community renewal as a mission for the community college:

> *The time has come to look beyond the conception of extension service, community schools, community service, and community-based education which has presumed their goal to be responsiveness to the learner and the community. What is needed now is a goal that includes not just responsiveness to needs but leadership in the improvement of all aspects of community life. Beyond being community-based, our colleges must now aim at human and community renewal* (Gollattscheck et al. 1976, p. 6).

They go on to suggest that the community college should be committed to improvement in all aspects of community life and should move beyond age barriers, degree structures, and credentialism toward urban renewal, environmental renewal, political renewal, and even moral and spiritual renewal.

Gleazer, an earlier advocate of community-based education, was arguing by 1980 that the community college should serve as the nexus of a community learning system, linking educational and cultural institutions, labor organizations, businesses and industry, public agencies, and civic organizations.

One cannot, of course, obtain a sense of the scope or patterns and practices of community service defined as community renewal. Neither can one properly assess whether community college activities in fact contribute to the "renewal" of communities. At present, the emphasis on community renewal appears to be primarily rhetorical.

But perhaps it is time to pause and ponder the rhetoric. Cohen and Brawer (1982) have asked and attempted to answer some important questions: "What stimulated these calls for completely revised structures? What made these advocates so concerned with community building and noncampus forms?" (p. 197). They suggest that the answer lies in the nature of political and fiscal support for community colleges. Community colleges depend entirely on public monies awarded in the political arena at both local and state levels. They must seek grass-roots support to compete with more prestigious universities.

TABLE 3
COMMUNITY SERVICE PROGRAMS AND ACTIVITIES
IN COMMUNITY COLLEGES
(Percentage of 173 Respondents)

	Educational Institutions			County Governments		
	Public Secondary Education	Community Education	Public Postsecondary Education	Recreation/Parks	Libraries	Aged
Type of organization						
Tax supported*	94	92	88	100	78	90
Not tax supported*	6	5	9	—	20	10
Both*	—	—	2	—	1	—
Not reported	—	3	—	—	1	—
Frequency of cooperation						
Continuing	27	76	65	69	78	70
Occasional	72	21	35	27	22	30
Not reported	1	3	—	4	—	—
Type of arrangement						
Credit course*	39	26	29	15	13	15
Noncredit course*	17	24	16	42	24	18
Community forum	4	3	8	4	3	3
Other program	22	18	24	12	41	48
Facilities only	14	—	15	23	16	9
Both*	4	29	6	—	3	6
Not reported	1	—	2	4	—	—
Nature of arrangement						
Joint sponsorship	53	71	59	38	44	58
College sponsorship	30	24	16	27	31	18
Community group sponsorship	11	5	7	31	8	15
Multiple sponsors	4	—	14	—	11	9
Not reported	2	—	3	4	6	—
Funding source						
Grant	4	—	8	—	8	9
Tuition or fees	46	66	36	19	38	36
College service	35	24	30	42	37	24
Other source	10	8	22	35	10	30
Not reported	4	3	5	4	7	—

Local/State Clubs and Organizations			Community Groups			Federal Government		
Performing	Civic	Recreation	Churches/Religious Organizations	Senior Citizens Centers	Community Centers	Military Total	Energy	HEW
10	5	7	2	43	16	99	62	100
90	87	94	98	35	78	1	33	—
—	5	—	—	—	4	—	—	—
—	3	—	—	22	2	—	4	—
40	45	49	66	86	64	68	29	58
54	52	46	33	14	36	32	57	42
6	3	5	1	—	—	—	14	—
6	10	4	6	27	12	49	10	17
8	13	15	18	30	30	15	14	17
7	12	4	3	—	4	2	19	33
33	26	13	43	35	28	20	19	—
42	34	62	28	5	26	11	29	17
2	2	—	1	3	—	4	5	17
1	2	2	—	—	—	—	5	—
25	30	16	24	19	54	55	29	67
26	16	14	52	76	32	21	14	8
34	40	58	19	—	12	13	14	17
6	9	4	2	5	2	9	23	8
8	5	9	—	—	2	19	—	
1	2	3	4	5	6	2	14	42
21	18	23	15	49	32	52	19	25
45	52	54	71	43	60	27	14	8
19	22	13	6	3	2	17	33	17
12	6	6	3	—	—	2	19	8

	Municipalities/ Local Governments			State/ Regional Governments		
	Corrections	Administrative	Recreation	Employment	Education	Corrections
Type of organization						
Tax supported*	100	91	96	98	97	98
Not tax supported*	—	6	4	2	2	2
Both*	—	3	—	—	2	—
Not reported	—	—	—	—	—	—
Frequency of cooperation						
Continuing	80	64	75	67	64	83
Occasional	20	36	25	32	34	17
Not reported	—	—	—	2	2	—
Type of arrangement						
Credit course*	39	15	6	26	22	59
Noncredit course*	32	6	21	5	20	19
Community forum	—	6	2	11	7	2
Other program	25	42	44	37	19	10
Facilities only	5	21	22	16	27	3
Both*	—	3	6	2	3	6
Not reported	—	6	—	4	2	2
Nature of arrangement						
Joint sponsorship	61	52	45	61	46	54
College sponsorship	35	24	41	7	17	16
Community group sponsorship	—	12	12	11	25	5
Multiple sponsors	5	12	2	14	8	14
Not reported	—	—	1	7	3	11
Funding source						
Grant	2	6	3	9	22	14
Tuition or fees	34	33	20	26	14	40
College service	45	27	61	39	37	22
Other source	16	24	14	18	15	19
Not reported	2	9	2	9	12	5

Private Enterprise			Unions			Occupational/Vocational		
Transportation	Real Estate	American Institute of Banking	United Auto	Plumbing	AFL-CIO	Hospitals	Vocational Education	Child Care
10	7	4	—	7	—	27	80	25
90	12	96	100	83	100	69	18	62
—	81	—	—	—	—	3	2	11
—	—	—	—	—	—	1	—	1
44	62	86	63	100	50	84	80	54
39	38	14	38	—	—	15	20	35
17	—	—	—	—	50	—	—	12
29	35	71	63	33	50	56	41	55
17	28	16	—	67	—	13	20	6
10	3	—	13	—	—	2	9	4
20	16	7	—	—	—	7	14	23
7	12	1	25	—	—	17	12	11
—	6	4	—	—	—	3	5	—
7	1	—	—	—	50	1	—	1
56	58	71	50	67	50	46	50	65
15	28	19	25	33	—	47	34	23
5	9	4	25	—	—	4	7	5
7	3	4	—	—	—	1	7	4
17	3	1	—	—	50	2	2	—
2	1	—	13	—	—	2	5	8
34	67	67	50	83	50	49	45	40
27	24	23	38	—	—	20	27	22
12	6	10	—	17	—	16	12	15
24	1	—	—	—	50	13	12	15

Source: Jamison Gilder and Jessica Rocha, "10,000 Cooperative
Arrangements Serve 1.5 Million," *Community and Junior College Journal*
(November 1980): 16–17.

In the last few years, some state legislatures (which provide from one-third to one-half of the funds for community colleges) have shown an unwillingness to pay for certain activities and have reemphasized transfer and vocational education. This change has led to the extensive relabeling of activities and to shifts from noncredit to credit offerings. It is too soon to know, however, how much actual service activity has thus been eliminated.[6]

Cohen (1977) and Cohen and Brawer (1982) have challenged the "noneducative" aspects of community renewal. Although Cohen supports the community orientation of community colleges (1969; Cohen and Associates 1975; Cohen and Brawer 1982), he has become increasingly critical of community service activities masked as education that bear credit but involve linking, brokering, and presenting rather than teaching and learning.

> *The real difference between college as a place of learning and community education as a concept is not between serving youth and serving adults, not between academic and vocational programs, not between the serious and the recreational. It is between curriculum and presentations* (1977, p. 20).

Cohen thinks community colleges ought to stay in the college business and concern themselves with learning and curriculum and grading and teaching.

> *Any public agency ultimately can be supported only as long as the public perceives its value. Each noneducative function may have a debilitating long-term effect, as it diffuses the college mission. The educative aspects of community education—its short courses, courses for institutionalized populations, and courses offered on job sites—are its strengths. Each time the colleges act as social welfare agencies or modern Chautauquas, they run the risk of reducing the support they must have if they are to pursue their main purpose* (Cohen and Brawer 1982, p. 282).

[6]Although it is related to the issue of public service, a discussion of the complex topic of community college finance is beyond the scope of this paper. See Breneman and Nelson 1981, pp. 160–94, for an excellent discussion of state and local finance of community colleges and their service activities.

Despite this view, however, it seems likely that the trend toward closer relationships with community groups, more diversified activities, and a stronger service orientation is likely to continue in community colleges. Community colleges seek and are likely to play a pivotal role in meeting the production-related imperatives of a high-technology society. They are powerful models of community service for other colleges and universities.

The community college is of course not the only institution providing community service. Continuing education, adult education, lifelong learning programs, and a host of special services—conferences, seminars, technical assistance, cultural and recreational events—are also provided by other colleges and universities, public and private. The extent or range of such activities does not appear to relate to the type of institution or the form of control, although public institutions appear to have more "free" services and the amount of service varies to a considerable extent with the size of the institution. Some distinctions can be made, however, by the type of community being served by colleges and universities. A special literature has developed around urban service and to a somewhat lesser extent around rural service.

Service to Urban Communities

An institution located in an urban area and an urban institution differ greatly, it has been argued. Many colleges and universities are located in urban areas, but there are many fewer urban institutions. Mayville (1980) defines urban institutions as "public service, community-oriented institutions" (p. 1). While such institutions predate the 1960s, their current sense of urban responsibility was greatly influenced by the social upheavals in big cities during that period and by the social programs initiated by federal, state, and local governments in response. During the 1960s and 1970s, several urban problems gradually developed: urban blight, high unemployment, high crime, shortages of housing, inadequate educational facilities, inadequate medical facilities, and lack of effective urban planning (Mayville 1980). Urban institutions have committed themselves to helping solve these urban problems as part of their service mission.

Urban institutions include public and private universities like the City University of New York (CUNY), Rochester, Pittsburgh, and Cincinnati; campuses of state systems located in urban areas like the University of Massachusetts–Boston or the University of Illinois–Chicago Circle; public and private colleges like Point Park in Pittsburgh; and a host of community colleges like Miami-Dade Community College. The most visible and largest urban institutions are those constituting the Committee for Urban Program Universities, which had 31 major university members in 1980. Additionally, two of the large national associations of higher education have specially organized their urban member institutions; the American Association of State Colleges and Universities (AASCU) has a network of 280 such institutions across 38 states, and the National Association of State Universities and Land Grant Colleges includes an urban division. AASCU's Urban College and University Network publishes *Connections,* a monthly journal full of descriptions of actual programs and discussions of the special problems of urban services.

Urban-service institutions serve their respective cities through educational, research, and direct service programs and through social problem solving. They are concerned with the special needs of urban students, which often means students from lower socioeconomic and educationally disadvantaged backgrounds and from minority groups. The Carnegie Commission on Higher Education (1972) argued that to adequately serve such students, urban institutions had to develop special academic support programs and to spend more money on entry-level students.

Many urban colleges and universities have followed the Carnegie Commission's recommendations, increasing their remedial programs and courses and developing a host of special programs (see, for example, Shroyer 1980 and especially volume 2, numbers 1 and 2 of *Connections*). Miami-Dade Community College, for example, has been described as "on the verge of achieving a breakthrough in pursuing quality in education without sacrificing open access" (Cross 1982–83, p. 12). Miami-Dade is a huge institution located in one of the nation's most troubled cities. It has an open admissions policy, and its diverse student body includes large black and Hispanic populations. According to Cross, Miami-Dade has combined comprehensive curricular reform, a redefinition of faculty roles to encourage more attention to advising and student development, and the use of technology to generate individualized assessments of progress for more than 400,000 students. The college sets standards, expects success, and has managed to obtain significant improvements from a large percentage of the student body.

Berube (1978) argues, however, that serving the urban student means not only open admissions but also free tuition. He thinks CUNY's free-tuition, open-admissions policies during the late 1960s and early 1970s were a noble experiment (both succumbed in the late 1970s to financial and political pressures) that a truly urban college should replicate. Berube argues further that existing colleges and universities do not match his vision of a truly urban college and that the federal government should intervene and establish a network of new urban colleges similar to the land grant institutions they created during the 1860s. (While his vision is perhaps overly ambitious, he nonetheless offers interesting perspectives on urban service.)

Concern with the urban student has another aspect to it as well, that of relating to the urban community's personnel needs. Berube notes that urban universities generally train a large proportion of the

> *bureaucratic manpower that operates the city's vital organs: the teachers, police, social workers, and other sundry civil servants who determine the quality of city policies* (1978, p. 13).

To a certain extent, urban institutions control economic opportunity for urban residents by controlling access to city positions. For this reason, it is particularly important for the urban institution to be committed to serving all members of the urban community.

Urban institutions are also concerned with curriculum. They attempt to bring urban issues and perspectives into the curriculum of established professional schools like education or social work and the established disciplines like sociology and anthropology. Several hundred institutions have created special, multi-, or interdisciplinary units of urban studies or urban affairs. Such units suffer from low prestige on the academic pecking order, however, and many have questioned the assumption that "urban" is unique and can be studied as such (Banfield 1970; Huber 1975).[7]

Beyond issues of clientele and curriculum, however, urban institutions serve in more direct ways through social action research and social problem solving. Many urban centers and institutes were created in the 1960s and 1970s with the explicit mission of community service. The Ford Foundation gave millions over the last three decades to universities

> *to encourage research on urban problems and to encourage closer contact between university scholars and city decision makers so research results could be translated into social action* (Pendleton 1974, p. 2).

The federal department of Housing and Urban Development (HUD) followed suit with the Urban Observatories Program, which provided a direct link between universities and city government and community agencies.

The University of Delaware provides a good example of an academic and service unit. With help from the Ford Foundation, the university created a Division of Urban Affairs in 1961. The original emphasis of the division was on helping solve urban community problems.

> *Unlike many other university units which started with such lofty goals and foundered as the academic community realized that it had taken on a load which it was not prepared to carry, the Delaware effort has flourished* (Phillips 1977, p. 45).

The University of Delaware was careful to recruit a faculty committed to public service, but the division began to offer academic programs as well. It is now a College of Urban Affairs and Public Policy offering masters and doctoral degrees in urban affairs and public administration. Faculty and students become involved in applied research and other service projects in close collaboration with community agencies through an urban agents program. Although they work with all kinds of local community groups, including governmental agencies, urban agents pay "special attention

[7]See Berube (1978, pp. 72–76) for a review and analysis of this debate.

to those groups which would not ordinarily have access to the services of the university" (Phillips 1977, p. 46). They try to work with community groups so as to help them become organized and self-sufficient. Although it has now expanded its focus to include service to state agencies and the state legislature, the college remains a model of urban community service.

Other urban affairs programs and centers have not been as successful as Delaware's, and many disappeared when the Ford Foundation and the federal government stopped providing special support for them. They had set an important precedent, however, and the idea of urban service is by no means dead. Title XI of the 1980 Amendments to the Higher Education Act of 1965 authorized a new program, the Urban Grant University Program. The purpose of this program, like Ford's and HUD's earlier efforts, is to encourage the application of university skills and knowledge to the solution of urban problems. The program authorizes the appropriation of escalating amounts of money ($50 million in 1981, $70 million in 1982, $80 million in 1983, $90 million in 1984, and $100 million in 1985) to fund projects in which universities and local government agencies collaborate. The act defines urban communities as those with over 500,000 population. While these monies have been authorized, they have not yet been appropriated, so it remains to be seen how much will actually be spent on the Urban Grant University Program. Still, congressional intent to support urban service is evident in this legislation.

Thus, community service is big business. It is a major aspect of the community college, where it takes a variety of forms and has many relationships with the educational program. It has taken on a special meaning in urban America, although it is by no means exclusive to urban institutions. In a service-oriented society, institutions of higher education remain actively involved.

College and university service to state and local governments involves some issues that are different from those associated with community service: What is the appropriate relationship between the educational/scientific and the political communities? What are the service responsibilities of public institutions toward the governmental entity— state, county, or municipal—that provides the major source of support? Can colleges and universities serve government without becoming servile? In what ways do colleges and universities differ from state and local government agencies, and what are their responsibilities toward them? Given that state and local legislative bodies and executive agencies are usually involved with complex policy and social problems, what are the responsibilities of colleges and universities for social problem solving?

These questions and controversies are not new. They have been debated since the early days of the republic. As noted earlier, the land grant movement, including experiment stations and extension services, that evolved from 1862 through 1914 and the Wisconsin Idea of the early 1900s established powerful and long-lasting models of service to state and local government. Each involved different conceptual formulations of the relationship between higher education and government and different answers to these questions.

Since the late 1960s, the trend has been toward closer connections and stronger service relationships. Many have voiced concern for the consequences, however, fearing the politicization of colleges and universities and the loss of independence essential to fulfillment of the essential roles of teaching, objective inquiry, and social criticism. Despite these concerns, however, the amount of public service activity increased in all types of colleges and universities.

Seven distinct types of services offered by colleges and universities to state and local governmental entities are identified in the literature: contract research, reference services, assistance in drafting legislation, testimony at hearings, training sessions, seminars, and exchanges of personnel (Phillips 1977). In a study on land grant and state universities, the most common types of services included contract research, training sessions, and seminars (Phillips 1977). The least common were exchanges of personnel, assistance in drafting legislation, and testimony at hearings.

It is probable that in other types of colleges and universities such specialized services are less common.

This section examines the issues and questions related to service to government, first from the perspective of state governments and second from the perspective of colleges and universities.[8] It then describes patterns and practices and provide examples of services.

State Government and Service

In the federalist system of government fashioned by Madison, Hamilton, and Jefferson, the states were given responsibility for the basic human needs of the American people—for education, health, recreation, transportation, culture, and security (Bebout 1972). Over the years and especially during the last four decades, the federal government, assigned to promote the general welfare, has used its taxing powers and its willingness to incur debt to provide extensive resources for and to become heavily involved in each of these areas.

Can colleges and universities serve government without becoming servile?

> *Even though the role of federal grants in financing state and local expenditures has increased greatly since the turn of the century . . . state and local governments retain a crucial role in the policy process. The increase in grants reflects . . . the effort of the federal government to improve the quality of decisions made by state and local governments. . . . Even at the height of federal interventionist strategy, state and local governments still continued to have the principal decision making role in the areas which they traditionally dominate* (Bebout 1972, p. 13).

The philosophy of the "new federalism" reaffirms the responsibilities of the states and shifts more of the burden of financing human services back to the states.

State governments have changed dramatically over the decades to meet the challenges of human service. "The recent rates of growth of state and local government em-

[8]Specific treatment of the relationship between colleges and universities and county and municipal governments could not be found. Many studies, while focused primarily on state government, cover local government as well, and it is probable that many of the issues and problems are similar.

ployment have exceeded those of both the federal government and the private sector" (Schneider and Swinton 1979, p. 12). Twenty states underwent "major" restructuring of their executive branches between 1965 and 1975 (Garnett 1979). Most states have increased the power of the executive branch, giving governors more power over state policy and the distribution of resources. State legislatures have become better organized, with more efficient committee systems and larger staffs (Folger 1980). State agencies have become more professional. State administrators in 1974 as compared to 1964 had achieved higher educational levels, were more representative in terms of age, sex, and ethnic origins, had more pronounced urban backgrounds, and were more professional with a greater orientation toward policy management (Wright, Wagner, and McAnaw 1977).

Despite these changes, however, state governments are very nearly overwhelmed by exceedingly complex problems in all areas of human service. A deteriorating economic situation in many states simply compounds the difficulties of state governments and reduces new and vitally needed sources of state revenue. A current list of problems facing state and local governments might include deteriorating transportation systems, environmental blight, scarcity of land and water resources, health care for the elderly and unemployed, decaying infrastructure in urban areas, and inadequate educational systems.

The major case for college and university service to government from the perspective of government, then, is simply that the intellectual resources in colleges and universities can be tapped to help solve these problems. Many elected and appointed officials would argue that, at least for public institutions, help with state and local problems *should* be a major responsibility of those institutions and that colleges and universities have an explicit obligation in return for the financial support given them (in most states, now the largest single item in the state budget). While politicians recognize that colleges and universities have other missions and responsibilities and are for the most part willing to treat them differently from other branches of government, they are impatient with images and attitudes reflecting the ivory tower.

It should be noted, however, that very little empirical evidence exists on the attitudes of state officials toward college and university service. While the situation has improved recently, very few studies are available.

The Council of State Governments (1972), a voluntary organization of the states, expressed concern over the lack of strong and effective interaction between higher education and state government, noting, "As a rule, state universities are given low marks by officials in weighing their contributions to the practical problems of [state] governance" (p. 4). They argued for serious efforts toward improvement on the part of colleges and universities and greater use of higher education by state government.

While all governmental entities need help with solving problems and with policy (Bebout 1972), the literature suggests that differences are apparent by type of governmental entity. The focus of the governor and the governor's office is usually on broad problems and issues of policy. Studies of economic developments and their impacts on the state and of trends in human service are in great demand and short supply. In many states (California and North Carolina, for example), the governor has developed a direct relationship with the public colleges and university for policy studies.

State agencies most often require technical assistance, analyses of policy, and special help with training, implementation, and evaluation. "Generally, governmental units are not able to afford the full range of technical personnel necessary to develop new procedures for dealing with day-to-day problems" (Scott 1974, p. 22). Most technical advice is provided through sponsored research projects or through consultation. Murray (1975) listed the agencies in Illinois most directly involved with higher education through sponsored research, among them the Board of Higher Education, the Division of Vocational and Technical Education, the Department of Labor, the Department of Public Aid, the Department of Transportation, the Department of Public Health, the Department of Children and Family Services, and the Department of Corrections (p. 239). A number of other agencies, boards, and commissions in Illinois had service relationships with colleges and universities as well. It is likely that a similar list would apply in each of the 50 states.

One of the rare empirical studies examined the relationship between state government and higher education in 14 southern states using mailed questionnaires and interviews (Henry 1976). The study included the governor's office, the legislature, and 14 functional areas covered by state agencies (environment, human resources, etc.). State officials turn to each other or to private consultants for professional consultation most of the time, but "a remarkable 95 percent of the officials have used or are using services of the academic community 'occasionally' or 'often' " (Henry 1976, pp. 100–101). Interestingly, state agencies in the South used training and educational services rather than advice on policy, planning, procedures, or administration (p. 101). Few state agencies had a formal policy regarding the services of colleges and universities. Half of the state agencies responding felt that college and university services were adequate but could be improved, while another 25 percent felt that universities were providing "the best service that could be expected" (p. 101). When asked about their needs over the next five years (from 1975), state-level administrators said that they would need training and educational services, and help with environmental concerns, long-range planning, and growth policies for state government.

State legislatures are concerned with formulating policy in human services and with decisions concerning allocation of resources. Often the debates and decisions involve trade-offs among the various human services. State legislators need policy analyses and "state of the art" studies from colleges and universities to help them identify alternatives and to assess the consequences of various options. The literature contains an extensive debate, however, on whether policy analyses can remain objective and supportive to political decision making or whether the analyses themselves become politicized in the process. Essentially, the debate is over the use of research results in policy making and over the value of policy research. Many in academia argue that policy research and policy analysis cannot remain sufficiently objective and free from political influences and that diverting research in this direction in the long run will be counterproductive to the development of knowledge and of sound policy.[9]

[9]See Schneider and Swinton (1979) for a review of some of the limitations of policy analysis for state and local governments.

Feller et al. (1975) studied the sources and uses of scientific and technical information in state legislatures and found that legislators prefer to use information generated internally by central or committee staff members rather than information generated by external sources. While Feller (1979) advocates improved linkage mechanisms between higher education and government, he also believes that:

> *The most effective long term improvement in legislative capabilities to analyze complex issues is likely to revolve around the development of internal legislative staff services, which, either by themselves or through their ability to communicate with the academic community and other research institutions, can provide information which is accessible, relevant, and comprehensible to state legislators. Universities cannot provide these services on a continuing basis. It would be unfortunate if the move to expand the public service role of universities became a substitute for legislative reforms, or if the universities active in such settings did not recognize or accept the fact that their "relative" role is likely to decrease over time (p. 149).*

Since 1975, state legislatures have become more active in developing service relationships with colleges and universities, and a variety of linkage mechanisms have been developed.

Higher Education and Service

During the last decade, colleges and universities of all types have shown a renewed interest in service to state and local governments.

State universities have the longest tradition and the most extensive service relationships. The many professional schools in state universities have developed close working relationships with state, county, and municipal agencies over the years, and they continue to explore new opportunities for applied research and service. Professional schools have always viewed socialization into public service as an important function. Countless institutes and centers with research and service missions have been established within professional schools (and even within arts and science departments) to strengthen contacts with state and local agencies. For professional school faculty, public service is seen as quite a legitimate activity, although in recent years some have begun to decry the overly theoretical orientation of professional schools and the retreat from concern with professional practice (Lynton 1982).

State universities have also established many multidisciplinary, free-standing institutes and centers that are intended to focus research and service in areas of social and human need (the environment, urban planning, public policy, for example). Many of them are creations of the late sixties and seventies, however, and have limited resources and precarious futures. Many state universities have also set up campus- or universitywide offices of public service to help link the resources of the university with the needs of external agencies. In some cases, they are combined with continuing education or extension units; in others they are entirely separate.

State universities have taken to documenting their service activities and to calling more attention to them as part of public relations campaigns. For these institutions, service is not only an important part of their missions but also an important part of their justification for increased resources. Other public institutions (for example, four-year colleges, teachers' colleges, and community colleges) follow the lead of the state universities, although the absence of extensive graduate and research programs limits their contributions in both contracted research and training services. They too, however, have attempted to document their service activities and have sought greater visibility for them in recent years.

It appears that independent colleges and universities are also eager to expand and take credit for their service activities, although this subject is discussed little in the literature. John Silber, president of Boston University, even claims that there is no distinction between public and private colleges and universities, only between publicly and independently supported institutions (1976). In his view, both types of institutions serve the public through education, research, and service programs. Publicly supported institutions are subsidized by the state for doing so, while independently supported institutions are privately subsidized for their public services. One need not—and many do not—agree with Silber to note, however, that many faculty members in independent colleges and universities perform a variety of services for state and local governments through research contracts and consultation. Their institutions have found it increasingly convenient to take credit for their actions. Such activity parallels the trend toward state support of the independent sector and a renewed interest in the question of whether or not we can or will afford to maintain our current diversified system of higher education with many independent colleges and universities.

So from the perspective of colleges and universities, then, service to state and local governments is increasingly perceived as an important obligation, important as well for the maintenance of a strong and viable resource base. Beyond this link, many professional schools and departments view service relationships as important adjuncts to the academic program, providing opportunities for education and research for faculty members and students alike. Most administrators and faculty members would insist that service to state and local governments need not and should not conflict with the primary obligations for teaching, research, and scholarly inquiry and with traditions of independence from state and local government.

The renewed interest in service to state and local governments is reflected in the fact that since 1972, five major conferences have been held on the subject at the universities of Illinois (1972, 1978), Georgia (1974), and California (1974) and at SUNY–Albany (1976). While the University of California conference was for administrators and faculty members in that system, the others brought together representatives from colleges and universities throughout the country. Papers and proceedings from these conferences are an important source of information on developing attitudes toward service and on state and institutional practices.

Much of the literature on service to state and local governments is descriptive and anecdotal. Only a few studies are based on information from a number of states and institutions. The Henry study (1976) noted previously was seminal in that it gathered information from state officials as well as college and university representatives. That report emphasized the attitudes of state officials toward academics and warned that attitudinal and procedural changes were needed for improved service relationships.

Bramlett (1974) also studied service to state government in southern states. Noting that no single approach is best for providing service and that each state would have to develop a structure suitable to its unique needs, he nonetheless offered a set of principles to guide decision making in this area:

1. Initiative rests with the university.
2. Not all schools should participate.
3. Elaborate linkage systems are expensive and unstable.
4. University commitment is essential.
5. Some level of permanent funding is needed.
6. Organizational structure should fit the need.
7. Just internal rewards are needed for service personnel.
8. Competent leadership and personnel are required.
9. Involvement solves the problem of coordination and orientation.
10. Political entanglements are avoidable in organized service programs.
11. The potential to influence public policy is earned.
12. The best advertisement is good performance.

A later work describes "representative" approaches in southern states (Bramlett 1976, pp. 50–61).

In 1976, Ione Phillips, working under the sponsorship of the National Association of State Universities and Land Grant Colleges (NASULGC), surveyed service to state and local governments by NASULGC's members. (NASULGC's members are among the largest institutions in the country and have the most extensive service missions.) The survey consisted of interviews and mailed questionnaires. Respondents included 79 of 133 NASULGC members and represented 41 of the 50 states. Respondents provided information on organized university units established especially to provide advice to governmental agencies, organized research institutes and centers whose activities related to areas of major public interest, types of services provided to state and local governments, levels and types of governmental entities being served, and perceived barriers and impediments to cooperative relationships between state universities and state governments. (Findings are reported throughout the following section on patterns of service.)

Worthley and Apfel (1978) also used questionnaires (130 officials in 32 states) and interviews (seven states) to compile a list of impediments and barriers to state government service. While barriers had been discussed in earlier literature, theirs is the most complete list:

- *A lack of compatibility between the more urgent needs of legislators and executives for practical and applied solutions and the university norm of emphasis on basis research and theory building;*
- *A reluctance on the part of state officials to believe that universities are capable of providing meaningful assistance and a reluctance on the part of universities to believe that their contributions will be valued and implemented;*
- *The lack of an effective information network for the identification of areas in which universities might be of assistance and an inability on the part of universities to identify and marshall a team of qualified personnel within the response time required by government;*
- *Difficulties with . . . [releasing faculty] to work on a particular project;*
- *The segmented nature of university organization, which makes interdisciplinary research difficult;*
- *A reluctance on the part of university faculty to become embroiled in the "world of politics" based on the assumption that such involvement would violate their professional norms of objectivity and independence;*
- *A faculty reward system that bases tenure and promotion on criteria that generally exclude applied research and consulting with state government;*
- *A lack of agreement on whether universities should work for state government as a service or for a reasonable consulting fee, i.e., as a means of supplementing faculty income or as a part of the public service mission of the university;*
- *The lack of recognized publishing outlets for scholarly writings based on applied research;*
- *The conflict between the frequent need of government for confidentiality of studies and results and the values*

of the university to generate and disseminate knowl-
edge and to remain apolitical;
- *A lack of understanding by academics and government*
  officials of the environments and procedures of the
  other;
- *The concern of government staff that university faculty*
  might supplant them (pp. 611–12).

Worthley and Apfel also described, from the literature, several recent attempts to provide links between universities and state government. Noting that "generalizations are difficult to draw due to the lack of systematic data on linkage attempts (especially evaluation studies) and on real differences in conditions among states" (pp. 615–16), they proceeded to make several observations that are similar to Bramlett's principles offered in 1974: involve both sides from the beginning; do not rush to formalize; expand the faculty reward systems; and develop dialogue (pp. 616–17).

Patterns of Service to State and Local Governments
The literature contains little information on patterns of service to state and local governments and reveals no preferences as to organizational approaches. Many have noted that the "best solution" will vary with the specific traditions, structures, attitudes, and policy problems in each state (Bramlett 1974; Phillips 1977; Worthley and Apfel 1978). "The most effective programs have one characteristic in common. They have been conceived to meet the unique political, social and technological needs of the areas they serve" (Phillips 1977, p. 172). Most authors suggest, however, that some form of linkage between higher education and government is desirable. Many states have created a formal "linkage entity" attached to the legislature or the governor's office. Many institutions of higher education, particularly the state universities, have created some organizational unit or specific mechanism to monitor and coordinate governmental service activities, even though many of these units do not have management responsibility for the activities. This approach appears to be consistent with preferences expressed at the state level. In the Henry study (1976), 60 percent of state officials suggested that universities ought to create a "nerve center" staffed and funded specifically to aid state government (p. 102).

Seventy-nine institutions responding to the Phillips survey (1977) had a formal unit whose major purpose was to match up "university expertise with governments' need to know" (p. 18). The most common approach was a technical services unit within an organized research institute or center, an "Institute of Government," for example. This institute would conduct research on state and local problems, while the technical services unit would provide linkages and short-term applied research. A few universities did not have a separate technical assistance unit but assigned the service function to the institute or center. A few others had both research institutes and technical assistance centers but treated them administratively as separate entities. Most of the technical assistance units were created during the 1970s. The units had widely different levels of available resources—annual budgets from $10,000 to well over $1 million—and staff size—from 1⅓ to 350 staff members. Most units, however, were quite small and had precarious funding (Phillips 1977).

While the literature is light on information concerning patterns, it is long on examples of specific practices. The following examples of statewide units, systemwide mechanisms, centralized campus-based programs, and decentralized approaches were selected from the literature as exemplary rather than representative.

... state officials [suggest] that universities ought to create a "nerve center" ... to aid state government.

Exemplary Approaches
Statewide
The state of Florida and the statewide University System of Florida have developed a program known as STAR, Service Through Application of Research (Bramlett 1976; State University System 1982).

The purpose of STAR is to encourage and enable state universities and community colleges to undertake specific kinds of research that are related to important public problems, particularly those problems that are of concern to state and local government and their agencies (State University System 1982, p. 1).

In the mid-1970s, the Research Priorities Advisory Committee, composed of legislative, gubernatorial, and university representatives, established statewide research priorities (Bramlett 1976). The priorities were broadly based and included such areas as natural resources and environmental management, social and rehabilitative services, and personnel and employment. The STAR program was created, given a direct state appropriation, and assigned to the SUS (State University System) Institute of Government for administration.

Each year the Institute of Government asks governmental entities to identify and describe significant problems and research needs relative to their particular area of concern. The institute circulates the lists of problems and research needs throughout the state university and community college system, and faculty researchers respond with specific project proposals and requests for funding. Each of the research projects must be a "cooperative endeavor involving a state university or community college, a unit of state or local government, and the SUS Institute of Government" (State University System 1982, p. 1).

The governmental agency and a special panel of readers review and evaluate proposals. A list of approved projects is developed and funded as part of the STAR program. In 1982, four projects were funded in the area of governmental operation, four in the area of natural resources and environmental management, six in the area of the economy and economic development, two in education, and one in crime control. The average project budget was $25,000; the total allocation for all projects in 1982 was $461,600 (State University System 1982, pp. 2–5).

The House of Representatives in Pennsylvania has established LORL, the Legislative Office of Research Liaison. LORL links the legislature, primarily the House but on occasion the Senate as well, with a number of cooperating universities—Pennsylvania State University, the University of Pittsburgh, Temple, Lincoln, Drexel, and the University of Pennsylvania (Feller 1979). A small core staff in the state capital whose salaries are paid by the House of Representatives is supplemented by faculty members contributed by the cooperating universities on a rotating basis. In addition, each university identifies a faculty member or administrator to serve as the liaison person on the campus. Inquiries are routed to and from LORL through the liaisons on each campus, and responses from more than one university to a single request are routed through LORL for "translation" and compilation as necessary. Most inquiries can be answered quickly and faculty members donate their time, but the occasional project that requires longer-term research is funded through LORL.[10] LORL has served as a model for many other states.

Systemwide

The University of California established a systemwide office of university public service in the mid-1970s to help coordinate efforts to fulfill the university's service mission. The office first identified the state governmental sources of policy research and technical assistance and initiated a series of briefings with the heads of state-level units. It also convened an all-university faculty conference in 1974 on applied and public service research (Jones 1979), which reaffirmed the service mission and called for more carefully delineated policies and procedures. The president of the university then designated an individual on each of the nine university campuses to serve as the point of access to university resources for that campus and as part of a universitywide network, coordinated by the systemwide office. In 1975, the university began a new initiative to provide an incentive for faculty research on state policy problems. The California Policy Seminar (Institute of Governmental Studies 1982) is a University of California/ state government program that seeks to match the state government's needs with universities' research capabilities by sponsoring faculty research projects.

The seminar is chaired by the president of the university; the 17 members include the governor, the speaker of the Assembly, the president pro tempore of the Senate, and appointees from executive branches of government, the Assembly, the Senate, university faculty, and students. Another 13 associate members also participate.

During its first years, all projects were for two years, and six new projects were funded each year. In 1982, however, the seminar decided to reduce the number of two-year projects to four and to sponsor a number of short-term projects as well. Members also changed the process for

[10]Another program, PENNTAP, links the multicampus Pennsylvania State University system with other units of state government, primarily state agencies.

selecting projects. The directors of the Assembly and Senate offices of research and the governor's Office of Planning and Research identified the major issues for California in the next five years. From that list of issues, the seminar formulated ten questions, including the following five:

1. *Assuming that no additional money is available, how should the public education system be changed to reduce school dropouts and increase the number of youth who either go on to college or become employed?*
2. *Should we expand or contract the responsibilities of counties, cities, and special districts, giving local governments more/less taxing authority, more/less control over various service functions? If we do nothing, what is the likely future of local government?*
3. *Consider the state's economic development and role in international trade.*
4. *Are there new ways to think about taxation in California?*
5. *How should the state deal with the often antiquated highway and personal transit systems?* (Institute of Governmental Studies 1982, p. 4).

Faculty members develop specific research projects to answer the questions and submit them for possible funding. During 1982, the research budget for the seminar was $340,500, while the administrative/dissemination/publication budget totaled another $100,000 (p. 17).

The University of Tennessee, a multicampus university system, has a systemwide Institute of Public Service (IPS) (Bramlett 1976; Phillips 1977). The institute includes several service units, among them the Municipal Technical Advisory Service, the County Technical Advisory Service, the Center for Government Training, the Environment Center, and the Transportation Center. The institute's mandate is "to coordinate and promote the University's assistance efforts for cities, counties, state government, business and industry (Phillips 1977, p. 32). It has regional offices throughout the state and comprehensive responsibilities in the area of public service.

Funding for IPS comes from a variety of sources, including direct state appropriations, federal grants, and appropriations from county and municipal governments. The budget totals several million dollars annually, and some years have seen funding problems. However:

the coordinated approach taken by the University of Tennessee is really unequalled by any other university. While a few other state and land-grant universities are spending roughly the equivalent amount of money for a wide range of government public service activities, none have coordinated their efforts under one umbrella to the extent achieved by IPS (Phillips 1977, pp. 35–36).

The California and Tennessee examples represent centralized, systemwide approaches. Although Illinois and Wisconsin have multicampus university systems, their approach to service to state government is decentralized. Both provide interesting examples of positive decisions in favor of decentralization.

In 1972, the Institute of Government and Public Affairs at the University of Illinois sponsored a national conference on public service to explore the problems and possibilities for the university's involvement with state and local government (Gove 1979; Gove and Stewart 1972). In 1973, the institute sponsored a local conference to address the question of whether it should serve as the principal conduit for research and other services to state government, and a self-study of existing relationships and contracts. The president of the university established the Committee on State-University Relations, consisting of faculty members and administrators from all campuses and the medical school. The committee was charged with examining existing relations "with a view toward seeking ways to improve the academic contribution toward solution of the State's problems" (Gove 1979, pp. 74–75). After a year of study, the committee and the university decided that existing research contracts and other forms of involvement such as conferences, seminars, and colloquia, service on boards and commissions, and student internships were proving satisfactory to all concerned and should continue unimpeded. The Institute of Government and Public Affairs did not need to take responsibility for service relationships, and no other centralized unit was needed. The committee did make a number of specific recommendations, however, related to compensation policies, evaluation, internships, exchanges, and the like that were intended to help strengthen relationships with state government. The committee also recommended that it become an ongoing committee to serve as a clearinghouse for requests from state officials lacking direct contacts within the university and to continue to examine the university's policy and practices in this area.

The University of Wisconsin also favors decentralization. Penniman (1979) notes the strong tradition toward service in Wisconsin and the fact that there has never been a period without research, technical assistance, and/or consulting between faculty members and state officials. The most common vehicle for providing service is a very large extension program, but the professional schools and many other units are involved as well. For the most part, individual faculty members are contacted directly, but the graduate school, deans, directors of centers and institutes, and the chancellor all provide referrals to individual faculty members when needed. Penniman argues that the "university needs a reference structure that will help identify contacts, but a single unit may impede rather than assist" (p. 55).

Campuswide

The University of Georgia is a statewide system of higher education with 31 campuses under one Board of Regents. A board-approved policy statement makes each institution responsible for public service, and service activities are organized differently on the various campuses. One large unit on the University of Georgia–Athens campus, however, provides the bulk of state government service (Bramlett 1976). The Institute of Government encompasses continuing education, technical assistance, and research services for all branches of government. Its activities include a wide range of services—staff development; programs and research projects in public safety, transportation, consumer protection, natural resources, legal assistance, and agricultural marketing; and educational television coverage of state legislative sessions. Many of the service projects and activities are provided at no cost to the state agency by postsecondary service units that are state and/or federally funded for such purposes. If teaching faculty are used, the state agency may be required to reimburse the institution for any substantial amount of faculty time devoted to the project. Overhead or indirect costs are quite often waived or at least reduced for state agencies.

Thus, a great deal of activity attests to the many different arrangements that can be made for providing service to state governments. Worthley and Apfel's observation (1978) continues to be true that little systematic data and even less evaluation information on links with state government are available, although many systems of higher education and many institutions have examined their own services to state government. As colleges and universities become more concerned with the ability of their states to provide needed resources, they are likely to continue to emphasize the service dimension.

Colleges and universities serve the business and industrial community, according to the more rhetorical definition of service, by producing graduates with the intellectual and technical skills necessary to become productive members of the work force. Using a more specific definition of public service, colleges and universities provide service through:

- The provision of credit and noncredit programs designed to meet specific needs for education and training of employee groups (e.g., insurance brokers, bankers, real estate agents). These programs are offered through continuing education and other academic units of colleges and universities and are usually made available at convenient hours and in accessible locations.
- The consulting of faculty members who help design and teach in the training programs offered by businesses and industries for their own employees. Many have called this the shadow educational system because of its size and rapid growth (Lusterman 1977).
- The consulting of faculty members who work on specific projects like testing materials and developing new accounting systems. Occasionally, special arrangements for leaves and sabbaticals allow faculty members to spend significant blocks of time at industrial sites.
- The scientific inquiry and research of faculty members and graduate students, which produces new knowledge that can be translated into new technologies, new products, and improved business practices. In most cases, such service is an unplanned by-product of ongoing basic research and instructional programs, while in others it results from specially developed projects, programs, and relationships.

While relationships between higher education and the business and industrial communities involving planned research have a long history, this form of public service also represents an exciting new area of interest and activity. The primary actors have been the major public and private universities (represented by member institutions of the American Association of Universities). Other universities and other types of institutions have been watching the development of closer connections with business and industry, however, and greater involvement with such forms of public service can be anticipated in the future.

Planned research partnerships benefit business and industry because they can lead to new technological innovations and allow the development of new products and other commercial opportunities. They benefit universities because they bring in new resources to support basic and applied research. They have been heralded as public service according to the following logic. The social benefits of a more productive business and industrial sector include a stronger economy, increased employment, and a higher standard of living. A more productive business sector can be achieved by the more expeditious transfer of new scientific and technical knowledge from universities to business and industry. The scientific and technical knowledge produced in universities, whether public or private, is made possible by public support from federal and state sources. Therefore, the university has the social responsibility to help business and industry through the transfer of technology and the application of research results (Bok 1982; Giamatti 1981).

This logic is not universally accepted, however. Relationships with business and industry have been criticized, also in the name of the public interest (Noble and Pfund 1980). Even when stronger relationships are advocated, there is widespread recognition that partnerships with business and industry involve inherent dangers to basic academic values and raise difficult questions of policy and procedure.

This chapter provides an overview of the issues and controversies, summarizing the advantages and disadvantages of cooperative research relationships. It also describes the various types of relationships between universities and industry and discusses several of the policy and procedural provisions that are considered important to safeguard academic interests. Finally, it includes several specific examples of current partnerships.

... there is widespread recognition that partnerships with business and industry involve inherent dangers to basic academic values ...

The Context for Partnership
The debate over the appropriate research and service relationships between universities and the business and industrial sector involves larger issues and trends in the economy, in science, in research and development, and in the process of innovation. It also raises questions about the

respective roles of the federal government, higher education, and the business/industrial sector. The research relationship has some problems:

[They] are deeply important problems, however, not because of the details or even the dollars but because they speak to how science is done. They speak to what the future holds for America's capacity to improve its productivity and economic vitality and to improve the quality of its citizens' lives through science and technology (Giamatti 1981, p. 132).

Concern was first expressed over the future of basic research and basic science in the United States. During the 1950s and 1960s, universities gradually assumed, and the corporate sector shed, the responsibility for the conduct of basic research (Smith and Karlesky 1978a). During the same period, the federal government gradually assumed, and again the corporate sector shed, the responsibility for financing basic research. This shift resulted from federal expansionist tendencies and from a weakening of the relationships between universities and industries. Those weakened relationships had several causes: (1) Researchers in industry and in academe were interested in different problems and slowly ceased to communicate; (2) students were interested in careers in academe not industry and thus did not provide the linkage they once had; and (3) industry had gradually shifted its emphasis from long-term basic research to short-term, applications-oriented research (Baer 1977; Smith and Karlesky 1978a, 1978b). Smith and Karlesky (1978b) argued that the interests of science and of research were better served by stronger partnerships between the university and industry, although the federal government would continue to be crucial as the major source of support for basic science.

Others made a similar case. The subordination of science and basic research to government had negative consequences:

As to government, there is now a strong tendency to judge science by what is politically expedient or politically fashionable; that is, to attempt to subordinate science, whether pure or applied, to value-judgments that

are the reverse of, and largely incompatible with, any
criteria one could possibly call scientific (Drucker 1979,
p. 807).

Drucker saw a shift in the values of both industry and
government toward immediate financially or politically
profitable solutions and a shift in the values of academic
science toward "neo-scholasticism" (p. 809). He argued
that these shifts were harmful both to American industry
and to American science. What was needed was greater
recognition of fundamental interdependence between
science and industry.

University presidents also began to be concerned about
excessive dependence on the federal government for
support of science. During the 1950s and 1960s, most
universities had built large research enterprises involving
large expenditures for personnel, facilities, and equipment.
They required ongoing financial support from the federal
government as well as new infusions of resources to remain
current with scientific developments and new instrumentation. Although federal support for research and development in universities increased 3 to 5 percent per year in
constant dollars throughout the 1970s (National Science
Foundation 1982, p. 1), federal priorities seemed to swing
dramatically and federal regulatory activity increased. The
situation appeared very unstable, and prospects for the
1980s did not look good. University presidents looked for
other sources of financial support and rediscovered business and industry.

At a meeting in Pajaro Dunes, California, attended by the
presidents of five major universities (Stanford, California
Institute of Technology, MIT, Harvard, and the University
of California) and a number of major corporate executives,
it was noted:

> . . . there is a genuine interest in facilitating the transfer
> of technology—from discovery to use—to contribute to
> the health and productivity of society; . . . dialogue . . .
> could improve the level of applied science by close
> association with industry applications; and academic
> institutions . . . are feeling hard pressed financially and
> see such cooperation with industry as a way of compen-
> sating for a small but important part of the support lost

from federal sources (Pajaro Dunes Conference 1982, pp. 2–3).

Business and industrial leaders, meanwhile, and those in the federal government concerned with broad economic trends began to emphasize high technology, the development of new products, and innovation as possible solutions to increasingly debilitating international competition and inflationary pressures.

Just as it needs educated employees, the business community must rely on the fruits of basic research for long-run prosperity and growth. The acceleration of technological advance has put a premium on innovative research and development leading to new and improved materials, processes, and products. . . . To an important degree, this process of innovation is made possible by the fallout from the basic research conducted on the campuses of colleges and universities (Smith c.1982b, p. 5).

Industries began to turn with greater frequency to universities for direct help. Industry support for research and development in universities grew approximately 7 percent per year in constant dollars between 1974 and 1979 and 13 percent in constant dollars between 1979 and 1980 (National Science Foundation 1982, p. 1). Although it must be remembered that industrial support for university research and development represents only a small portion of the research budget in most universities, it is likely to continue to grow and to become more significant.

Some, however, take a different view on the merits of this collaboration. Noble and Pfund (1980) argue that university/industry connections pose a threat to university autonomy and independence "at a time when we need to rethink fundamentally the central economic and political questions of modern industry and democracy" (p. 252). They also see a threat to the principles of science and research in the "ethically murky world of dual alliance to science and to profit" (p. 252). In their view, big business is co-opting the university, through research contracts and other forms of support, to join in its long-standing campaign against government regulation. They see discussions of innovation, technology transfer, and most recently, risk, as academic subterfuge masking the important battle against regulation. Finally, they see the transformation of "part of a public-sector social resource into a private-sector preserve, with little public scrutiny or accountability over its use of the facility" (p. 252).

Although most observers in the end do not agree with Noble and Pfund, they do acknowledge that many difficult issues and problems are raised by university-industry research relationships (Baer 1980; Bok 1982; Brodsky, Kaufman, and Tooker 1980; Fusfeld 1980; Kiefer 1980; Latker 1977; Prager and Omenn 1980; Rosenzweig 1982; Roy 1972). Most serious is the potential for conflict with the university's basic obligations to scholarly inquiry, research, teaching, and social criticism and the related threat to the independence of higher education. Observers recognize that certain complex problems are related to secrecy in research, faculty and even institutional conflicts of interest, policy regarding personnel, and the right to intellectual property.

These problems have been discussed extensively over the last several years. Special commissions and study groups have been established: the National Commission on Research established in 1978 and sponsored by a variety of organizations, including the American Council on Education, the American Council of Learned Societies, the Association of American Universities, and the National Academy of Sciences; the Business–Higher Education Forum established in 1978 by the American Council on Education; and the Committee on Government-Industry Relationships created by the National Academy of Sciences. The issues have been debated at the annual meetings of several scientific professional associations, including the American Physical Society, the American Chemical Society, and the National Academy of Engineering. Many conferences and symposia during the last three years have attracted large numbers of university administrators and faculty members (for example, "Cooperative Research Mechanisms for Synergistic Interaction" sponsored by MIT and the National Science Foundation in 1980, "Successful Models of University-Industry Collaboration on Research" sponsored by the American Association for the Advancement of Science in 1981, "Science, Education, and Industry: A Joint Endeavor" sponsored by the American Society for Engineering Education in 1981, "Can the Law Reconcile the Interests of the Public, Academe, and Industry?" sponsored by the Association of the Bar of the City of New York in 1982, and "Partners in the Research Enterprise: A National Conference on University-Corporate Relations in Science and Technology" at the University of Pennsylvania in 1982).

What has emerged is a general, although by no means universal, consensus concerning the advantages and the disadvantages of cooperative research relationships between higher education and the business and industrial community and a broad delineation of roles and responsibilities of universities, the corporate sector, and the federal government (see table 4).

Rosenzweig, in a more recent study of the issues (1982), pointed out additional advantages. He noted that partnerships with business and industry allow universities to diversify sources of support and reduce dependence on the federal government. The quality of scientific instrumentation in university laboratories does not match that in industrial laboratories, and access to modern equipment is an important benefit. He advocates closer relationships because he considers the advantages to outweigh the disadvantages.

The presidents of major universities (Bok 1982; Giamatti 1981; Pajaro Dunes Conference 1982), the National Commission on Research (1980), the Business–Higher Education Forum, many heads of businesses and industries, and officials in the federal government (David 1982; Kiefer 1980) also advocate closer relationships. They do so in the name of increased resources and in the interest of public service and social responsibilities.

Hence a university should properly pursue these opportunities both for its own self-interest and because every institution that depends on public support should recognize a responsibility to serve society's legitimate needs (Bok 1982, p. 166).

Forms of Partnership
According to Baer,

consulting and the exchange of people (e.g., an industrial scientist serving as a visiting professor, or a faculty member spending a summer or sabbatical in industry) are the most direct ways of linking academic and industrial research. They are probably also the most effective means of transferring knowledge between the two sectors (1977, p. 39).

Prager and Omenn (1980), drawing from Baer's description of the mechanisms that can encourage closer collaboration and from Roy (1972), summarize the types of university/industry relations (see table 5). They argue that

. . . a whole spectrum of university-industry interactions and relationships is possible depending on the goals and objectives of the respective organizations and their institutional characteristics. Relevant factors include: the size, structure, and profitability of the industry, the nature of its business, and the progressiveness of its research program; and the type, size, and financial health of the university, the relative size and stature of its science and engineering programs, and the orientation of its research and researchers. External factors such as geographic proximity, the location of university alumni in key industrial positions, and migration of university faculty to industry and vice versa may be very influential (Prager and Omenn 1980, p. 381).

Corporate contributions to universities, the first type of relationship on Prager and Omenn's list, represent a form of philanthropy that is different from support of research and development and is intended to be of direct benefit to the particular corporation. Even though it represents only a small share of college and university budgets, corporate philanthropy plays "an important role in ensuring academic quality and underpinning the diversity and independence of higher education" (Smith c.1982b, p. 3). Approximately 10 percent of corporate contributions to colleges and universities are directed to support of graduate students (Smith c.1982b), considered particularly important in an era of demographic decline and declining federal aid for graduate students. While the monetary value of corporate contributions is important, it should also be noted that

a well-structured program of educational support serves to create and maintain desirable relationships between

TABLE 4

BENEFITS AND HAZARDS OF COOPERATIVE RESEARCH

Benefits	Hazards	Roles and Responsibilities of the Partners
Universities		
1. Acquaintance with the marketplace and process of innovation	1. Inhibition of unfettered choice of research	1. Protection of the academic environment
2. Access to additional technical and physical resources	2. Temptation for more applied and development programs	2. Development of a cooperative research framework
3. Enrichment of the curriculum	3. Suspicion of use of university resources for private benefit	3. Need to ensure industrial contributions as part of relationship
4. Income from patent licenses	4. Polarization of opinion of special interest groups against universities	4. Need to inform university community of need and character of proprietary protections
5. Additional sources of funding for research		5. Provision of legal and policy guidance to participating faculty and students
6. Less paperwork and administrative burdens compared to direct government funding		
7. Enhanced public credibility for service to society		
Industry		
1. Opportunity to acquaint research students with industrial research environment	1. Loss of some control over a proprietary position	1. Provision of goods and services to meet public needs
2. Influence on future directions for research	2. Lack of relevance of university research to industrial problems	2. Development of mechanisms for transfer of research into the process of innovation
3. Source of new skills and techniques for re-	3. Suspicion of use of university re-	3. Commitment to

search
4. Opportunity to experiment more efficiently with new directions in research
5. Increased access to peer review
6. Generation of excitement and enthusiasm
7. Enhancement of public credibility

sources for private benefit

develop research ideas, sharing benefits with university
4. Provision of long-term research support
5. Provision of access to industry equipment and processes for participating university research personnel

Government (public interest)
1. Improved innovation's leading to long-term stable growth of the economy
2. More efficient flow of research knowledge into industry
3. Improvement of the science

1. Potential for monopolistic action or restraint of trade
2. Commingling of public funds for research with privately supported programs

1. Decreased barriers and provision of incentives for cooperation between universities and industry
2. Support of studies of potential problems in the relationship and development models
3. Support of cooperative research where public payoff is high
4. Development of long-term perspective for cooperative research programs
5. Provision of financial incentives for industry support of research in universities

Source: National Commission on Research, *Industry and the Universities: Developing Cooperative Research Relationships in the National Interest* (Washington, D.C.: National Commission on Research, 1980), p. 16.

TABLE 5
TYPES OF UNIVERSITY-INDUSTRY RELATIONSHIPS

Corporate Contributions to Universities
Undirected corporate gifts to university fund

Capital contributions: gifts to specific departments, centers, or laboratories for construction, renovation, equipment

Industrial fellowships: contributions to specific departments, centers, laboratories as fellowships for graduate students

Procurement of Services
By university from industry: prototype development, fabrication, testing; on-the-job training and experience for students; thesis topics and advisers; specialized training

By industry from university: education and training of employees (degree programs, specialized training, continuing education); contract research and testing; consulting services on specific, technical, management problems

Industrial associates (single university, usually multiple companies): payment of fee to university to have access to university's total resources

Cooperative Research
Cooperative research projects: usually basic, nonproprietary research involving direct cooperation between university and industry on project of mutual interest with each sector paying salaries of own scientists; may involve temporary transfers of personnel for conduct of research

Cooperative research programs: industry support of portion of university research project (balance paid by university, private foundation, government); results of special interest to company; variable amount of actual interaction

Research consortia: single university, multiple companies; basic and applied research on generic problem of special interest to entire industry with industry receiving special reports, briefings, and access to facilities, for example

Research Partnerships
Joint planning, implementation, evaluation of significant, long-term research program of mutual interest and benefit; specific, detailed, contractual arrangement governing relationship with both parties contributing substantively to the enterprise

Source: Denis J. Prager and Gilbert S. Omenn, "Research, Innovation, and University-Industry Linkages," *Science* 207 (January 25, 1980): 381.

*corporate and academic personnel . . . [and that the]
contacts facilitate the recruitment of new employees, the
interchange of technological information, and the
exchange of ideas, opinions and understanding . . .*
(Smith c.1982b, p. 3).

The procurement of services by business and industry
through training programs, consultant services, and short-
term contract research represents the second type of
university-industry relationship, according to Prager and
Omenn. Industrial or corporate associate, affiliate, or
liaison programs have proliferated rapidly over the last few
years (Smith c.1982b, p. 4). In exchange for a fee, the
industry or corporation usually obtains access to faculty
and students for consultation as well as access to seminars
and publications:

*Such programs give the corporate community an oppor-
tunity to monitor ongoing research, expose industry
scientists to new ideas, and provide early access to
students for recruitment purposes* (Smith c.1982b, p. 4).

MIT, CalTech, Penn State, Stanford, and Lehigh are
examples of universities with liaison programs. Although
particular arrangements vary, most programs operate
through established research institutes and centers.
Cooperative research programs, research consortia, and
research partnerships involve specific arrangements and
fees for the participating corporation(s) or firm(s). They can
be bilateral or involve more than one company and/or more
than one university. The scope and purposes of the research, the ownership of the research results, the disposi-
tion of profits, and other provisions are negotiated and
established in formal agreements. The many research
consortia and partnerships that have been established
during the past few years vary greatly, and no common
patterns and practices have developed. A number of these
provisions have been discussed extensively in the literature,
however, and because an enormous interest is apparent in
the higher education community in the development of such
partnerships, they are treated separately.

Special Provisions for Partnerships

The special aspects of research agreements and related issues that have received the greatest attention in the literature include secrecy, rights to intellectual property, and free publication; patents, patent-licensing, royalties, and exclusive licenses; faculty responsibilities and conflicts of interest; and university sponsorship of commercial ventures. While no formulas are available, a consensus appears to be growing on general principles and safeguards that are important to higher education in each area.

University presidents and corporate leaders attending the Pajaro Dunes conference in 1982 identified secrecy as the major difficulty associated with research agreements and partnerships. While recognizing that the desire for competitive advantage naturally leads business and industry to opt for as much secrecy as possible, both during the research and when results are available, they also agreed that secrecy can:

> *harm the progress of science, impair the education of students, interfere with the choice by faculty members of the scientific questions or lines of inquiry they pursue, or divert the energies of faculty members . . .* (Pajaro Dunes Conference 1982, p. 5).

While they avoided dictating specifics, they recommended that careful attention be paid to these issues in the development of research agreements. They suggested that the agreements themselves might be made public and/or subject to review by faculty bodies to ensure consistency with academic values and further that universities should be careful to avoid excessive restrictions on the disclosure of information, although a "brief" delay in publication to allow for processing a patent would be acceptable.

Much of the literature reaffirms the value of patents and patent licensing as a legitimate incentive for translating discoveries into useful products, a process that protects the rights of the inventor *and* promotes the progress of science and technology (Baer 1980; Bok 1982; Pajaro Dunes Conference 1982). Universities have had policies regarding patents for years and have recently become more aggressive in seeking patents for faculty members' inventions. An important development is the recent change in federal law allowing universities and small businesses to have title to inventions resulting from government-sponsored work, which is intended to promote and facilitate the transfer of technology (Bok 1982). With respect to university-industry partnerships, however, patents and patent licensing raise a number of sticky questions: Who owns the right to seek a patent for inventions produced by university faculty research under corporate sponsorship? Should universities grant exclusive licenses or does exclusivity impede the transfer of technology? In exchange for corporate sponsorship, should universities give away the right to exclusive licenses for future patentable inventions?

Presidents and corporate leaders at Pajaro Dunes noted that the important principle involved in such issues is the desirability of developing the patent. Licenses should be awarded to those firms most likely to develop them, and exclusive licenses appear acceptable in those cases in which "exclusivity seems important to allow prompt, vigorous development of the patent" (p. 8). They encouraged universities, however, to allow exclusivity only for the amount of time necessary for such development, and they disagreed on the issue of the right to exclusive licenses for all future discoveries, noting that "the question needs to be addressed by universities on a continuing basis in light of their experience" (p. 9).

Research partnerships pose a variety of problems of conflict of interest for faculty members and their institutions. The most general conflict concerns faculty workload and time commitments, but other problems are related to teaching, advising of graduate students, other research activities, compensation policies, and direct conflicts for faculty with stock and/or managerial positions in research-related companies. The literature is full of reaffirmations of the primary obligations of faculty members: teaching, the development of new knowledge through research, and public service. Usually, research contracts, programs, and partnerships are considered consistent with these obligations. Regarding consulting arrangements for which faculty members receive direct remuneration, however, universities have developed a variety of policies regarding workload and reporting mechanisms to protect the institution and the individual. In response to other similar situations, institutions should take particular care not to influence faculty

Research partnerships pose a variety of problems of conflict of interest for faculty members and their institutions.

members in their choice of research topics and research directions, and faculty members should take particular care not to lead graduate students into projects and dissertation research that is responsive to corporate concerns but not in the students' best interests (Bok 1982; Pajaro Dunes Conference 1982). Institutions should not use compensation or other forms of faculty rewards (e.g., promotion, reduced teaching loads, more office space, better laboratory equipment) to improperly direct faculty research toward areas that would prove lucrative to the university (Bok 1982). And when faculty members hold stock or managerial positions in companies whose principal activity is research and the companies seek research partnerships with the university, the institution must be particularly careful to avoid favoritism and role conflicts with faculty (Bok 1982).

Perhaps the most controversial topic is the question of whether universities, in collaboration with faculty members, should take an active part in the formation of research-related companies to gain financially from the venture. Faculty members, particularly in the field of biotechnology, where it is assumed that large profits are possible from new discoveries in the near future, have formed companies and sought university sponsorship, offering a share of the profits in return. A number of major universities have flirted with such possibilities. Throughout 1981, Harvard considered such a venture, under the watchful eye of the press, and finally decided against it (Bok 1982). Such commercial ventures can lead to a variety of administrative conflicts and difficulties, and

> *they inevitably change and confuse the relationship of the university to its professors. The faculty member who joins with the administration in founding a new company is no longer valued merely as a teacher and a scholar; he becomes a significant source of potential income to the institution. . . . This new role immediately casts an aura of ambiguity and doubt on many decisions that the administration regularly makes* (Bok 1982, p. 161).

Affected decisions could include those involving tenure, promotion, salary, workload, laboratory space, and equipment. Bok argues further that such commercial ventures promote unwanted secrecy, endanger basic academic values, and divert the university into excessive concern for profit at the expense of the leadership in science and research that is their obligation and particular responsibility (p. 165). University investment in such faculty ventures

> *is not advisable . . . unless they are convinced that there are suficient safeguards to avoid adverse effects on the morale of the institution or on the academic relationships between the university, its faculty, and its students* (Pajaro Dunes Conference 1982, p. 11).

Because each university-industry agreement or partnership develops from a unique set of interests and purposes, their specific provisions will differ. Conferees at Pajaro Dunes and others (Baer 1980; Bok 1982; Prager and Omenn 1980) agree, however, that while each university must develop its own policies and procedures, each should address the difficult problems and potential conflicts "vigorously and make efforts to publicize widely and effectively the rules and procedures it adopts to avoid compromising the quality of its teaching and research" (Pajaro Dunes Conference 1982, p. 12).

Working Examples: Research Partnerships; Consortia; University, Industry, and Federal Initiatives
The descriptive literature on university-industry research partnerships has grown during the past several years. From this literature, the following examples have been selected to illustrate the variety and scope of partnerships. They include two bilateral agreements, two agreements involving one university and several companies, two agreements involving multiple universities and companies, and several arrangements initiated by a university, by industry, or by the federal government.

Harvard-Monsanto
The Harvard-Monsanto agreement is a long-term research partnership in the area of biological and medical research. According to the charter agreement, Monsanto provides the funds ($23 million over 12 years, starting in 1974) and the technology. The research is determined and conducted by Harvard scientists at Harvard laboratories, although some Monsanto researchers work in parallel in their own laboratories. Harvard researchers are free to publish their findings

and patent their results, while Monsanto has the right to develop commercially any medical materials that result from the research. Monsanto has the right to exclusive licenses on patents for a limited period of time. An advisory board, made up of outsiders to both Harvard and Monsanto, has been established to review and "safeguard the public interest" (Bok 1982; Prager and Omenn 1980).

Several distinctive features characterize the Harvard-Monsanto agreement: the focus on a new scientific area, sufficient researchers in one university interested in the new area, a willing industrial partner with a research program but not interested in developing basic research competence in the new area, and long-standing personal relationships among the scientists (Prager and Omenn 1980).

MIT-Exxon

The MIT-Exxon agreement is similar in type to the Harvard-Monsanto partnership but different in some interesting respects. It is a 10-year, $7–8 million agreement focusing on combustion research essential to the development of more efficient fuels. In contrast to the Harvard-Monsanto agreement, MIT scientists obtain research funds by submitting specific project proposals for review and selection by Exxon. By agreement, however, MIT can use up to 20 percent of the total funds for those combustion studies it considers important. MIT can patent the research results, while Exxon has a nonexclusive royalty-free license to use the patents. Exxon and MIT share license fees from other users (Kiefer 1980). According to Kiefer, the MIT-Exxon ingredients for success include "direct people-to-people relations and extended support" (p. 48).

MIT Polymer Processing Center

This example of a cooperative research consortium is also an example of successful and appropriate federal involvement in university-industry collaboration. The center was initiated in 1973, primarily with National Science Foundation funds. It is now supported by industry at ten times the original budget. It involves twelve companies (including General Motors, Eastman Kodak, and Xerox), who support basic research projects on polymers.

Funding from each company varies with the company's size and volume. While regular technical review meetings are held for university and industry representatives and an advisory committee made up of industrial participants has been formed, there is little other direct industrial involvement in the center.

MIT selects the research projects, which are performed primarily by participating graduate students. Many faculty members are involved with the center as well, however. MIT encourages publication of research results and owns all patents resulting from the research. MIT can choose to award licenses to any company, whether or not that company is part of the agreement, but it shares royalties with member companies (Kiefer 1980).

The center's success has been explained in terms of leadership, faculty involvement, and educational orientation. It is in the education mainstream at MIT and enjoys strong participation from faculty and students (Kiefer 1980).

Leadership is the most important factor in success. You need a university person, preferably well-respected, mature, with industrial experience, and academic tenure, to take charge. But the university itself also must really want the institute, as well, and be willing to commit space and some money and to reward the professors who are involved. There must be no doubt about the academic quality of the research. Finally, of course, it is necessary to have industrial firms who are likewise committed— willing to provide funds, maybe $50,000 to $100,000 each per year, for a sustained period (Robert Colton quoted in Kiefer 1980, p. 43).

Center for Integrated Systems—Stanford
The Center for Integrated Systems is currently being established at Stanford, following the MIT Polymer Processing Center model. Seventeen microelectronics firms are contributing $12 million to construct a new building and support research in electronics.

An interesting feature of this arrangement is that the center's corporate sponsors will be entitled to have their own scientists on site full-time, thereby providing them with virtually unprecedented access to graduate students and academic research in progress (Culliton 1982a, p. 961).

Research Triangle Institute and Park

The Research Triangle Institute is a nonprofit research consortium established with state government support in 1959 by the University of North Carolina, North Carolina State University, and Duke University. It oversees Research Triangle Park, which is a large research facility. Private companies (Airco Industrial Gases, Data General, for example), professional associations, and staffs of university research projects rent space in the park. More than 40 research enterprises occupy space on park grounds. The purpose of both the institute and the park is to improve relationships between research-intensive industries and sponsoring universities (Brodsky, Kaufman, and Tooker 1980). A board of governors composed of university, corporate, and state government representatives formulates policy for the institute.

Research Triangle Park has become the model for state government support of the academic-industrial connection.

> *Industrial parks offer easy access to a widely differentiated resource base. But the degree to which participating firms and universities take advantage of the opportunity for knowledge transfer undoubtedly varies* (Brodsky, Kaufman, and Tooker 1980, p. 62).

Center for Biotechnology Research—Stanford

The Center for Biotechnology Research is a nonprofit organization financed by Engenics, a newly formed company created by a Stanford faculty member. Engenics in turn is financed by six major corporations (Bendix, General Foods, Koppers, Mead, MacLaren Power and Paper, and Elf Technologies) (Culliton 1982a). The center provides two scientists—one at Stanford, the other at the University of California–Berkeley—with research support approximating $2 million over four years. Both scientists are performing basic research on the development of chemical processes using genetically engineered microorganisms.

Engenics has the rights to commercially useful research, but the Center for Biotechnology Research has a 30 percent equity interest in the company.

> *This unusual nonprofit/for-profit union was pioneered by Stanford as a way of putting organizational distance*

between the university and the corporate world that is
supporting university research (Culliton 1982a, pp.960–
61).

University of Pittsburgh CAST and FAST
The University of Pittsburgh has started two new
programs—CAST and FAST—"to enhance the effectiveness of its research interface with the industrial sector"
(University of Pittsburgh 1982, p.1). The Center for Applied
Science and Technology (CAST) is a university center
whose purpose is "to provide the environment and the
essential linkages to promote and nourish the process of
technological innovation" (p. 1). CAST programs usually
involve the government as a partner with the university and
industry. The Foundation for Applied Science and Technology (FAST) focuses on the same objectives as CAST but is a
separate corporate subsidiary of the university.

Established in 1982, FAST provides a more flexible
vehicle for the management of large-scale research ventures
"of the type in which the university can expect to participate as equity partner in the research results" (p. 1). The
initial plans for FAST include the development of the
capability to conduct research in membrane exchange
devices and potential projects in the development of absorb-
ents, gaseous sterilants, and a genetically differentiated
strain of beef cattle.

The university plans to use royalties and other equity-
derived revenues from FAST projects to create a research
endowment for the support of basic research and research
in the social sciences and humanities.

Both CAST and FAST programs focus on activities
ranging between conceptual innovation and proof of technological feasibility. The university considers it inappropriate
"to participate in development or marketing. . . . It does,
however, encourage industry participation on campus to
create [the] linkages required to assure smooth transition to
the industrial setting" (p. 2).

Council for Chemical Research
The Council for Chemical Research is a unique example of
an industrywide effort to support chemistry and chemical
engineering research. Consisting of industry and university
representatives, the council has established a special fund

with contributions from chemical firms. The purpose of the council, still in the development stage, would be "to provide colleges and universities with new, significant, and continuing sources of funding for basic research of potential value to the chemical industry" (Kiefer 1980, p. 49). Other goals are to promote collaboration between industries and universities, to encourage innovation, and to promote the education of science and engineering professionals. Grants from the fund are to be made to worthy research projects in any university. Rosenzweig (1982) is encouraged by the industrywide collaboration in support of higher education and sees the model as potentially adaptable to other industries. He warns, however, that:

> *it is important to be thoughtful, while the relationship is still in the formative stages, about the policies that are most likely to be successful and the conditions that are most likely to produce these policies* (p. 45).

The current federal role with respect to university-industry partnerships can perhaps best be described as "facilitative" (Prager and Omenn 1980; Rosenzweig 1982). Although a number of federal agencies (e.g., Defense, Energy, Commerce, Transportation) have specific programs designed to support university-industry collaboration in areas considered to be in the national interest (Prager and Omenn 1980), the National Science Foundation (NSF) has been the most active. A new Division of Industrial Science and Technological Innovation was established in 1981; its purpose is to:

> *increase cooperation between universities and industry, stimulate technological innovation and commercial applications in small businesses, and stimulate adoption and use of research results by industry and long-term collaboration between universities and industry* (National Science Foundation 1983, p. 45).

The Cooperative Research Project
The Cooperative Research Project is designed for research on fundamental, scientific, and engineering questions. Proposals, submitted jointly by a university and industrial

researcher, undergo normal NSF peer review, but they are judged on the basis both of scientific quality and the likelihood of effective collaboration between university and industry researchers (Kiefer 1980, p. 43). A central pool of NSF funds is dedicated to this program, but funds from other NSF divisions are used as well. NSF funds are used to cover the university's share of costs, while industries are reimbursed a portion of costs on a sliding scale (larger companies receive next to nothing, smaller ones close to 100 percent). The National Commission on Research (1980) identifies this policy as a weakness in the program "because large companies possess the largest number of excellent researchers who can work with university researchers most effectively" (p. 22).

Some examples of projects funded under this program include a Bell Laboratories–Lehigh University project on thermal convection in cavities, a silicon structures project involving CalTech and several computer firms, and an Eastman Kodak–Clarkson College project on crystal formation in surfactant solutions (Prager and Omenn 1980, p. 382). Others involve Cornell and Hewlett-Packard; Stanford, CalTech, and Hercules; the University of Pennsylvania and General Electric; and Cornell and Atlantic-Richfield (Kiefer 1980).

The Cooperative Research Centers Program
Initiated in 1972, this program supports large-scale collaboration between universities and industries. At present there are a number of such centers: Furniture R&D Applications Institute, North Carolina; MITRE Energy Development Systems; the MIT Polymer Processing Center; and others at the University of Massachusetts, Rensselaer Polytechnic, Kent State University, Case Western Reserve, the University of Kansas, Ohio State, Worcester Polytechnic, and Catholic University.

Cooperative research centers focus on particular scientific areas and cover basic and applied research as well as generic technologies that might lead to new products, processes, or services. NSF and participating industries fund start-up costs, but centers are expected to become self-sufficient over time (Kiefer 1980; National Science Foundation 1983).

Small Business Innovation Program

This program funds high-risk research in small science and technology firms. The objective is to increase the amount of research on scientific and technical problems where the solutions promise substantial public benefits (e.g., advanced production and manufacturing techniques, deep mineral resources, advanced instrumentation) (Kiefer 1980; National Science Foundation 1983).

Despite the existence of many examples of cooperative programs and research partnerships between universities and business and industrial firms, it remains true that "little is known about the kinds of arrangements most likely to produce fruitful associations between universities and industries" (Rosenzweig 1982, p. 58). These agreements are generally too recent to have allowed for any form of evaluation or in-depth analysis, and none are found in the literature. Continued experimentation with different kinds of agreements and evaluative studies are likely in the future.

ORGANIZING FOR PUBLIC SERVICE

It is evident from the review of higher education's service mission and the ways services are delivered that colleges and universities are extensively involved in an impressive number and variety of service activities. What remains to be examined are the structures, policies, and procedures that have been developed within colleges and universities for the organization and delivery of public services. For some aspects, it is possible to generalize across all types of colleges and universities, but for others, the type of institution (community college, four-year college, or university) and form of control (public or independent) must be distinguished.

In contrast to the literature on the research and teaching missions in higher education, not much of the literature is devoted exclusively to the organization of and policy regarding public service. These subjects are discussed, however, in the more general literature on organization, structure, and finance of higher education and in the literature on service for particular client groups (for example, communities, state and local governments, business and industry). This chapter reviews the issues and practices related to structure, policy, patterns of activity and rewards, and resources for public service.

Organizational Structure

Organizational structures in colleges and universities are designed primarily to fulfill the missions for teaching and research. Academic departments, schools, and colleges are organized by subject areas, disciplines, or professional areas and by related fields to facilitate the production of knowledge and the teaching of undergraduate and graduate students. Administrative offices either support students and faculty members directly or research and teaching functions indirectly. Few organizational structures are designed specifically for the delivery of public services. In most cases, it is assumed that the public service mission will be fulfilled by the existing academic and administrative units. While service activities and subject areas overlap to some extent (for example, public health services, engineering services), there is usually no match between needed public service and the academic and administrative units in colleges and universities. This "lack of fit" has been identified as one of the major organizational problems of

Few organizational structures are designed specifically for the delivery of public services.

academic public service (Henry 1976; National Commission on Research 1980; Worthley and Apfel 1978). It is a problem that has been recognized for some time in higher education, however, and colleges and universities have dealt with it in a variety of ways. While many differences are apparent within the various types of institutions, general approaches tend to vary by type of institution.

Of all types of institutions, community colleges are most likely to have a specially designed service structure, but no uniformity is evident across institutions. Wygal (1981) discusses the diversity of organizational structures for community services in the community college, noting that this function has been the most dynamic feature of the community college during the past decade.

> *One may find at the community college an array of titles for community service administrators: vice presidents, deans, directors, coordinators, etc. At many colleges, the two words "community services" are not found in any title, but the function is performed by one holding a title such as "Dean of Continuing Education" or "Director of Community Education." And in other institutions, the community service function is simply an "add on" to another activity* (p. 3).

During the past few years, many community colleges have created a division or office of adult education or community education, but it remains to be seen whether this trend will continue. Such divisions or offices usually absorb existing community services units, which is consistent with the evolving definitions of community and service within the community colleges discussed earlier.

The literature contains no evidence concerning which designation or organizational unit is most effective for the delivery of community services in the community college. Wygal (1981) notes that "a wide range of successful community services programs may be found" (p. 3) with all types of organizational designations and that "the key to success in community services is not found in appellation; it is found in status—the importance placed upon it in the college" (p. 3). According to Wygal, status results from a great many interactive factors, including the commitment of state, local, and institutional leaders to the concept (expressed in public statements *and* in allocation of resources); status and rewards for community service leaders within the college; maximum involvement of faculty, students, and community leaders; and clear policies, procedures, and processes for the delivery of services (pp. 3–5).

Although many associated with community colleges complain that community service has not achieved the status it deserves within the college (Keim 1976; Vaughan 1980; Yarrington 1976), there is no doubt that community or public service has achieved greater organizational status and recognition in community colleges than in other types of institutions. Some community colleges and systems (Vermont Community College System and Coastline Community College in California, for example) have even experimented with noncampus forms as a way of "taking the college to the people."

With the exception of urban colleges whose service mission is distinctly urban, four-year colleges, whether public or private, do not appear to have a separate organizational structure for public service. Service activities may be performed within academic or other organizational units, but the literature contains very little on liberal arts or other four-year colleges that speaks to the service mission or to service activities. The literature contains some discussion about service learning (Martin 1977), accomplished by involving students and faculty members in off-campus service activities. A special campuswide office might help coordinate such activities, but service learning is usually closely affiliated with and supervised by academic departments and programs. Increasingly, four-year colleges are creating special units of continuing or adult education that serve older "returning" students and are sometimes described as public service activities (Cosand 1981). Faculty members in colleges are usually considered to be engaging in public service while acting as paid consultants for various organizations and groups (Silber 1976), and some faculty donate their services to civic and community organizations. These activities, however, are carried out within traditional academic units and structures.

Urban colleges, however, often have special academic programs in urban affairs or community services that combine teaching, applied research, and service (Berube 1978). They also often have a special office or individual responsible for acting as liaison with various community groups, for making arrangements for the use of facilities by community groups, or for linking faculty expertise and community needs (Berube 1978).

Public and private universities deliver public service through traditional academic departments and professional schools, but additionally thay have created institutes and centers within some academic units (Ikenberry and Friedman 1972). Institutes and centers are distinct organizational units with primary responsibility for research and/or for public service. Normally, institute and center directors report directly to a department head, a dean, or, for large interdisciplinary units, a provost; thus, they are tied to the academic heirarchy of the university.

Beginning in the 1950s, it began to be clear in universities that the academic department was not the best unit to carry out research and service programs, particularly those supported by grants and contracts (Ikenberry and Friedman 1972).

The creation of task-oriented, special purpose institutes and centers provides many grantors additional assurance that their resources will be used to pursue their goals rather than the general objectives of the university (Ikenberry and Friedman 1972, p. 14).

Ikenberry and Friedman favor institutes and centers because they allow for greater specialization in tasks. An additional advantage of centers is that they can bring together faculty members from a variety of disciplines, thus achieving a better fit between academic resources and public service needs.

Since the 1950s, institutes and centers have proliferated rapidly. More than 5,000 are listed in the *Research Centers Directory* (Thomas and Ruffner 1982), but they vary enormously. Some are quite large and prosperous and enjoy high status within the university, the state, and even the nation. Others are small and hardly visible except for their descriptions in brochures and catalogs (Ikenberry and Friedman 1972).

The difficulty of making clear distinctions between research, applied research, research services, and public services noted earlier is faced *within* institutes and centers.

An orientation toward research predominates in the natural and life sciences, while an orientation toward service predominates in the social sciences, the humanities, and the professional fields (Ikenberry and Friedman 1972). Most institutes and centers perform a mixture of research and service, however, and many are involved in education and training as well.

The best source of information on institutes and centers is the *Research Centers Directory* (Thomas and Ruffner 1982). The directory lists and describes all research centers in universities and other nonprofit research organizations, but it defines research quite broadly and includes centers and institutes engaged in both research and service. Each listing in the directory provides information not only on location, affiliation, and major purposes but also on activities, publications, and services.

Although it is difficult to generalize about institutes and centers, it is clear that they provide a great deal of university public service. They also provide an alternative to large, complex institutions for external groups seeking service (Penniman 1979).

Another organizational unit within universities concerned with the delivery of service is the continuing education program or division. Such units are also "task-oriented" (Ikenberry and Friedman 1972, p. 55); that is, they assemble information on educational and service needs and identify and coordinate university talent and resources to meet the needs, "but typically they do not provide the services themselves. Their primary function is to coordinate its [service] delivery" (p. 55). Continuing education units in most universities have grown dramatically throughout the 1970s and have greatly expanded their range of services. Many have become involved in the delivery of credit as well as noncredit programs. While they have become quite large, their status within the university hierarchy is generally believed to be quite low compared to more traditional academic departments, professional schools, and even centers and institutes. While regular faculty members teach in continuing education, especially for extra remuneration, they usually do not otherwise become involved. Community residents who are not regular faculty members, however, often become involved as teachers and resource specialists for continuing education programs. Many continuing education programs have found creative ways to take advantage of community, industry, and other resources. This extensive use of nonregular and part-time faculty for instruction has complicated organizational and personnel problems for continuing education programs and for their institutions.

Although four-year colleges and universities rarely have a centralized office of public service and prefer to decentralize this responsibility, multicampus systems often attempt to coordinate service activities among the various campuses within the system. The following list, for example, includes the functions of a systemwide office of university public service for the University of California. Similar functions are performed by similar offices in other multicampus universities.

1. Assemble and distribute inventories of university research projects and faculty expertise related to problems of significance to California.
2. Facilitate the coordination and support, systemwide and campuswide, of symposia, conferences, briefings, and consultations with university faculty, staff, and students on matters of major public concern for which there is an evident need.
3. Conduct discussions with the staff of all standing, joint, and select committees of the state legislature to determine information needs and to provide policy-related research results and technical assistance from university faculty and staff.
4. Sponsor and coordinate the preparation of monographs and other publications on specific subjects to provide a point of departure for the consideration of important issues by the state legislature and executive branch.
5. Coordinate a universitywide clearinghouse for public officials and government agencies to disseminate research information and to provide access to scientific and technical personnel.
6. Covene intercampus meetings on institutional processes and policy through which the university as a whole can better meet the policy development and research needs of the California state government.

7. Encourage and work with the Senate Committee on Research to develop policies to promote the use and application of university research in the development of state public policy.
8. Initiate contact with agencies of state and local government to inform them of the university's sources of expertise, including preparing and distributing information about the university's public service capabilities.
9. Assist the president's special assistant for governmental relations in identifying university faculty able to provide technical assistance to the California legislature.
10. Encourage the establishment of intercampus programs of research that promise to contribute to the solution of major state problems (Jones 1979).

Policy
Most colleges and universities proclaim a commitment to public service as part of their formal mission statement, but few have separate policy documents regarding public service. Institutional or statewide master plans usually state the service mission of the institution(s) in terms of the service region (the county, the city, the state) and describe a variety of service activities. For example, the master plan of the State University of New York (SUNY) states:

In addition to the pursuit and augmentation of those campus efforts which normally serve the respective communities, the University as a whole will mount a Statewide effort to identify the major public problems, at all levels, and the University capabilities which could best contribute to the solution of such problems, and bring about a still more direct mobilization of effort in terms of public service. The redevelopment of the economy and the maintenance of efficient and effective social services, for example, will be matters of major concern to the University (State University of New York 1978, p. i).

More specific policies affecting public service are distributed among a variety of other policy documents, such as faculty personnel policies and governance policies, and among institutional rules and regulations for such matters as workload, salaries, academic credit, the use of facilities, and so forth. For this reason, it is difficult to obtain a clear picture of public service policy for any one institution and impossible to generalize across institutions. Even where a distinct organizational unit for public service exists, the delineation of roles, responsibilities, functions, and relationships with other units is largely a matter of institutional traditions, norms, and personalities rather than a reflection of policy.

Gradually, however, a few tacit and quite general agreements about public service have developed within colleges and universities:

- The institution has a publicly proclaimed mission of service, and faculty members are expected to help fulfill it. The "how" is left intentionally vague and is clarified only by individual negotiation within the various academic departments and other units (Bok 1982).
- "Faculty members have public duties such as other citizens and therefore will serve on many boards, commissions, and task forces without compensation, just as do public members" (Penniman 1979, p. 52).
- When faculty members speak out on political or controversial social issues, they are careful to separate their private opinions from official university policy (Bok 1982).
- A faculty member's primary responsibilities are to engage in research and/or to teach, depending on the type of institution, and he or she will not compromise the fulfillment of those obligations by excessive institutional or public service (Bok 1982).
- In public universities and public community colleges, faculty members have special responsibilities to state and local government and should provide a certain amount of "gratis" assistance. Services that require excessive amounts of time can be charged for. The determination of what is "excessive" is for the most part individually negotiated (Penniman 1979).

In recent years, a number of colleges and universities (primarily public institutions) have published descriptions and guides to their public service activities. While the purpose of such documents is generally oriented toward public relations, they occasionally contain important information on institutional policies and practices. *The Third Dimension* (State University of New York 1978) is an example. The stated purposes of the document are to make it better known that the university is serious about its service mission, to profile faculty members' special service capabilities, and to illustrate, through examples, the major kinds of public services available "so that . . . prospective clients can better understand the possible uses of the University's diverse resources" (p. i). It contains descriptions of 14 very diverse kinds of services, including training courses for local government personnel, a description of the New York Sea Grant Institute, a list of services to libraries and library users, and many more. Dividing the state into four regions, it lists specific programs, faculty expertise, and contact persons for each SUNY institution within the region. It also contains the following disclaimer:

> *This report* does not *pre-commit the availability of any and all capabilities of the University to any and all prospective clients at any and all times and places. It must be remembered that there are some deserving projects which cannot be sustained without special arrangements for special financial support, . . . and that the public service usage of University expertise must be kept in balance with the usage of that expertise for the other missions of the University—basic teaching and basic research for the advancement of knowledge* (p. ii).

Patterns of Activity and Reward Structures

Common wisdom holds that public service is not rewarded in academic communities, at least not nearly so well as research and teaching. Common wisdom also holds that because public service is not rewarded, faculty members are reluctant to engage in it. The common wisdom in both cases may be true, but little evidence is cited in the literature. Indeed, the literature includes very little at all beyond repetition of these "facts." Tuckman (1976) provides the most thorough analysis of reward systems and structures, showing that an academic reward structure does exist in higher education despite the fact that it does not reflect any intentional or stated institutional policy. Furthermore, according to Tucker, the reward system is usually clearly perceived by faculty members and does have an impact on their behavior.

It is also clear that patterns of structure and governance do influence the reward system. With respect to public service, the effect is not necessarily positive. The combination of an academic structure organized by subject specialty and a governance structure that decentralizes decisions about hiring, promotion, tenure, and in many cases salary to departmental faculties often means that skills and accomplishments in research and teaching carry greater weight than public service. In many institutions, and for many faculty, it matters little that presidents and board members proclaim the commitment to public service. What matters is what is given greatest weight in faculty committee meetings where tenure, promotion, salary, and merit increases are decided.

The initial decision, of course, concerns hiring. Given that colleges and universities include service among their three primary missions, it should follow that institutions would attempt to assemble a faculty competent in all three areas. They generally do not. Although faculty search committees (whose recommendations carry the major, and usually definitive, weight in such decisions) pay careful attention to accomplishments and potential for research and/or teaching, only in the most exceptional unit (the College of Urban Affairs and Public Administration at the University of Delaware, for example) is any consideration given to the potential for public service. This tendency results in part from who makes the decision and in part from the fact that it is difficult to judge potential for public service. How can a committee decide whether or not an individual is likely to be committed and active or able to work effectively with various external groups? Because it is difficult and seemingly more peripheral than competence in teaching and research, faculty committees, deans, and provosts usually ignore this aspect altogether.

Many institutions hire full-time specialists with skills in public service, just as they hire research specialists. In some institutions, such individuals are given faculty titles but are not included in the tenure stream. In others, they are considered nonacademic professionals. In hiring service specialists, universities look for evidence of ability to communicate effectively with various community groups, for special knowledge and expertise in the particular service area (for example, knowledge of legislative processes for legislative liaisons), and often for skill in policy analysis. Institutions appear reluctant to hire service specialists any more than absolutely necessary, however, because such decisions create difficult problems with personnel and resources for the institution. Colleges and universities therefore generally prefer to use regular faculty resources for public service. Despite this institutional reluctance, however, many universities are developing a professional subclass of service specialists. When this group is combined with research specialists, the numbers can be significant. Little research has been done on this group of professionals in higher education, however.

Determinations of workload also present difficult problems. The definition of "service" and "normal" research and/or teaching, advising, and committee activities varies widely among disciplines and professional areas. Most institutions, once they have established broad policies on teaching loads for graduate and undergraduate classes, simply leave all decisions about workload to the academic unit. The amount of public service is therefore usually determined by a combination of the faculty member's predilections and department heads' and deans' leadership and predilections. Most institutions ask faculty members to report their activities in teaching, research, and service by the semester or year, but often the forms provided for such purposes fail to distinguish between institutional service, public service, and service to the discipline or profession. How, or indeed whether, such self reports are used to evaluate performance remains idiosyncratic to each college and university.

A few colleges (Hampshire College, for example) have experimented with faculty growth contracts in which faculty members plan their activities in advance and are expected to specify to the extent possible the amount of time they will spend in various activities, including service. The contracts provide a basis for subsequent evaluations of performance. Theoretically, such systems could make it easier for faculty members to obtain prior endorsement for public service, and they could make it easier to document the scope of service. The number of institutions with growth contracts is

Despite . . . institutional reluctance, . . . many universities are developing a professional subclass of service specialists.

small, however, and the system has not been studied from the perspective of public service.

Promotion, tenure, and salary are the major rewards in academia. Depending on the type of institution, faculty members document accomplishments in research, scholarly activity, teaching, and public service as part of the process of review for promotion and tenure. Documentation of public service is required in all types of colleges and universities. Most people believe, however, that public service matters far less than other activities when it comes to the final decisions (Phillips 1977). As with decisions about hiring, the fact that faculty peer review systems are used suggests that public service accomplishments will be given less weight. Additionally, it is exceedingly difficult to find adequate measures to judge excellence in public service, even more difficult than judging scholarship and teaching. Based on what is not reported in the literature, it appears that efforts have not been made to tackle this difficult problem of measurement.

Somewhat more is known about faculty salaries and public service. Tuckman (1976) examined the relationship between faculty salaries and skills in publishing, teaching, public service, and administration. He performed a cross-section regression analysis using data on 53,000 faculty members collected by the American Council on Education in a 1972 survey. The faculty sample included full-time faculty members from 78 universities, 181 four-year colleges, and 42 junior and community colleges. Among the institutions, different levels of selectivity and wealth and represented. For the analysis of rewards for public service, Tuckman had to assume that involvement in public service was an indication of skill in public service because he had no other means of measuring or approximating skill in that area. A further problem with the study is Tuckman's definition of public service as service that "entails meeting with communities and public organizations, *working on departmental or university committees,* and performing charitable or educational activities" (p. 54, emphasis added).

Tuckman found that faculty members who were skilled in (that is, engaged in) public service did earn somewhat more than faculty members who were not (did not). The salary rewards for research skills were far greater in actual dollar amounts, however. Interestingly, the salary rewards were more significant for public service than for teaching.[11]

. . .Those engaged in public service receive statistically significant salary increments more frequently and in higher amounts than those with outstanding teaching skills. Nevertheless, they usually have lower salaries than those who publish (p. 76).

Tuckman further analyzed salary differences by academic area and found that public service was rewarded in engineering and mathematics and in physics and chemistry, but not in the earth sciences. It was not rewarded in the biological sciences. Of the two liberal arts disciplines he examined—English and music—it was rewarded only in music. Public service was rewarded in most social science disciplines but not in anthropology. Of the four professional areas examined—education, law, medicine, and pharmacy—it was rewarded only in education. Male faculty members earned a larger salary increment for public service than did females. This finding is worthy of note as women faculty members devote more time to service activities than do men (Riley, Baldridge, et al. 1978).

Tuckman (1976) distinguishes between constraints and incentives, noting that most institutions operate with a system of constraints—specific rules and regulations that prohibit or circumscribe behavior—because they are easier to develop and implement uniformly. Incentives to encourage desired behaviors are more difficult to design in higher education and are used less often. He argues, however, that incentives are more effective in producing desired behaviors from faculty members. Given the common wisdom among faculty about the low priority and negative rewards for public service, this observation suggests that colleges and universities who wish to emphasize public service will have to design a system of incentives to make it happen.

Resources

The area in which no clarity at all is apparent has to do with resources. Who pays for public service? Who should pay?

[11]For research and teaching, Tuckman measured skill by publications, teaching evaluations and awards, and a number of other measures.

For public institutions, what proportion of service activity should be considered to be already paid for as part of appropriations for state and local higher education? For private institutions, how much free service is owed to society?

Most public service activities are not specially or separately included in college and university budgets (Penniman 1979). They are performed by faculty and staff members as a normal and expected part of their jobs. This dispersion of responsibility throughout the institution may increase the amount of service, but it makes it impossible to develop an accounting system that measures the amount of institutional resources devoted to public service. Different definitions of service simply compound the problem.

In theory, the service activities performed by special service units can be accounted for by the size of those units' operating budgets. In practice, however, the budgets are usually a variable combination of internal and external, grant and contract resources, and they handle faculty time so variously that they do not present an accurate picture of resource allocations for service activities. For example, an institute with a formal budget of only a few thousand dollars may in fact call upon extensive and costly services of many faculty members. In some cases, departmental budgets may over-reflect and service units under-reflect faculty resources.

Practices involving external support for service activities also differ. For most service activities, the full costs, both direct and indirect, are charged to the recipient. For some public institutions, however, the indirect and occasionally some portion of the direct costs are waived for governmental or other public agencies (Bramlett 1976). While institutes and centers have a structural advantage for the delivery of services, they will not have the freedom to establish and pursue possible service relationships with many external groups if they depend on external sources for basic operating expenses (Feller 1979).

In community colleges, the changing definitions of what can be funded through state and local appropriations have caused enormous shifts in service activities. In California, the passage of Proposition 13 resulted in an estimated 60 percent decrease in budgeted public services, although it is impossible to tell how much actual activity was decreased.

Most colleges and universities consider paid consultancy by faculty members a service activity. Most institutions have rules about how much time can be spent on outside consulting, on how much extra income can be earned, and on how extra income is to be reported. These rules vary considerably from institution to institution, and there is no common standard for all of higher education or even for particular types of institutions (Penniman 1979). While institutionally imposed limits on outside consulting and externally earned income are intended to protect the basic functions of teaching and/or research, in practice they limit the amount of service activity. They also complicate efforts to account for the resources dedicated to public service.

While the faculty member gets paid for the extra time he or she spends as a consultant, the college or university is contributing resources to the activity in the form of faculty fringe benefits, office space, secretarial time, library and laboratory resources, and even computing and duplicating costs. The total dollar value of such contributions can be quite high. When the consultant relationship is with a community or governmental agency, the institution may well wish to contribute such resources as a public service, but when the relationship is with a corporation or consulting firm, it may not wish to do so. As Lynton (1982) asks: "When a professor turns consultant, what's in it for the college?" (p. 45).

[There is] an urgent need for mechanisms which would make faculty available on as flexible a basis as is possible under existing consulting arrangements, while yet assuring some indirect cost return to the institution (Lynton 1982, p. 45).

Lynton suggests the development of a practice plan similar to those used for medical school faculty, in which the institution collects a fee for service to the patient and reimburses faculty based on a sliding scale (p. 45). This system provides incentive and reward for faculty members and income for the institution. Lynton notes further that some engineering schools have begun to use the same type of arrangement as well and that it could be adapted to include instructional services (p. 45).

The literature provides scant evidence of efforts to examine and devise organizational structures, reward systems, and institutional policies on the allocation of resources and other matters that will enhance the public service mission and provide for the effective delivery of public service. At the same time, however, more thought and experimentation with incentive systems and rewards and with faculty growth contracts and practice plans hold some promise for the future.

SOME CONCLUDING RECOMMENDATIONS

The starting assumptions of this investigation of public service in higher education were that service is an appropriate and important mission for colleges and universities and that the identification of current issues and controversies related to, and patterns and practices of, providing service would supply information, ideas, and suggestions for those engaged in or contemplating service activities. It is time to reexamine those starting assumptions and to ask whether the patterns and practices of providing service shed any light on the mission as a whole.

It is clear from the literature that a great many people consider public service to be an important and appropriate mission—in fact, an obligation and a responsibility—for higher education. The concept and definition of public service entail enormous difficulties, however. As Laurence Veysey noted nearly 20 years ago, the concept of service is at once too broad and too narrow. It is so broad that nearly every activity in higher education can be, has been, and currently is labeled as service (at least by someone). If all research, scholarly, and educational activities are excluded from the definition, however, it can become so narrow as to describe nothing. Definitions of research and scholarly inquiry have expanded over the years to include a wide range of analytical and practical activities under the notion of applied research. Definitions of education and teaching have evolved to include lifelong learning, as well as active involvement in service activities as part of the learning process. We have seen from the literature that perspectives on what is appropriate public service differ according to different conceptions of higher education as a whole. They change over time as the clientele expands and more and more services become absorbed into normal research and teaching. At the present time, the perspectives are so various that it is very difficult to make any sense at all out of the concept of public service. Can anything be done to clarify the conflict? Four areas of further research are apparent after this review of the literature.

1. Investigate service as a mission. There is both too much and too little literature on public service in higher education—too much because the treatment of the service mission is contained throughout the literature on higher education and throughout the literature more specifically related to institutional types, and too little because very few

It is time ... to ask whether the patterns and practices of providing service shed any light on the mission as a whole.

books and articles treat the subject of public service in any depth. There is little research and theory on service and hence no developing body of knowledge on the service mission in higher education. More sustained analysis of the service mission in higher education *as a mission* is needed, as well as a more careful examination of the structures, policies, and practices for delivering service.

2. Analyze the role of community colleges in community service. The descriptive literature on particular forms of public service—service to the community, to government, and to business and industry—reveals different strengths and weaknesses and leads to different recommendations for further inquiry. It is difficult to separate the literature on community service from the literature on the community college. An enormous amount of effort has been expended in trying to define community service(s) and in extolling the virtues of the "community"-oriented college, but a tendency exists to substitute rhetoric and polemic for analysis of community service. While community colleges have undertaken an impressive array of community services and external groups generally perceive them as accessible, helpful, and cooperative, more analysis of this function is needed.

3. Evaluate arrangements for providing service to government. The literature contains ample description and commentary on service to state government. It is clear that many institutions are extensively involved in a wide variety of such activities. It is time now, however, to engage in more extensive analysis to determine which types of arrangements (special public service institutes, technical assistance centers, systemwide mechanisms for legislative liaison, for example) have proven to be most effective. Evaluative studies are particularly needed.

4. Develop a system for gathering and disseminating information about service to industry. The literature on service to business and industry reveals a relatively consistent and thorough sense of the issues, problems, and opportunities associated with the development of direct service relationships. Experimentation with different practices and mechanisms of delivering service continues. This area is developing rapidly, however, and it deserves careful attention to ensure that important academic values and obligations are protected even as opportunities are fully

explored. A system for gathering state-of-the-art information on developments as they occur and for disseminating information within the higher education community is desirable.

Lynton (forthcoming) argues that we should drop the notion of public service altogether and concentrate instead on adapting the missions of research and teaching to the current environment and context of higher education. Higher education would thus be more responsive to society's needs and demands. The argument has much merit. For one thing, it would eliminate the conceptual morass we now have. Unless and until the changes in research and teaching are accomplished as Lynton suggests, however, it will not be in the best interests of higher education to eliminate references to public service. Service is simply too important to our relationships with other societal institutions and too central to our claims for public support.

Colleges and universities are clearly fulfilling many obligations and responsibilities for public service, expanding activities in the areas of community and adult education, corporate education programs, and a variety of research and technical services. Even so, service providers need to examine their motives. Are recipients served because of a commitment to community service or as a means of maintaining institutional enrollments? The competition among institutions for funds from state and local governments and from private and corporate sources is masked by proclamations of the commitment to service as part of the justification for financial support.

Is it possible [however] . . . in our competitive quest for funds . . . that we are creating and presenting an image to the public, who support us with their tax funds, of self interest rather than community interest, and that our actions really exacerbate the problem of decreased financial support? (Cosand 1981, p. 5).

This question cannot be answered easily. The integrity of higher education must be maintained and false claims and promises in the name of service avoided.

The patterns and practices of providing service do not clearly tell us which kinds of service activities are most appropriate and best delivered by colleges and universities.

Different sectors of higher education and different institutions will want to design public service programs that reflect their unique traditions, environments, and priorities. And service activities will naturally vary according to the recipient. A review of current patterns and practices does reaffirm, however, the principle discussed repeatedly in the literature: that the most viable service activities are those most closely related to the "academic essence" and "the central purposes of teaching and research" (Carnegie Commission 1972, p. 4). Public service embodies important notions of a direct relationship between colleges and universities and external groups and a set of responsibilities and obligations toward a larger society. We must seek to clarify our concepts and delineate our roles and responsibilities. It will not be an easy task, but it is an important one for higher education.

BIBLIOGRAPHY

The ERIC Clearinghouse on Higher Education abstracts and indexes the current literature on higher education for the National Institute of Education's monthly bibliographic journal *Resources in Education*. Most of these publications are available through the ERIC Document Reproduction Service (EDRS). Publications cited in this bibliography that are available from EDRS include the ordering number and price at the end of the citation. Readers who wish to order a publication should write to the ERIC Document Reproduction Service, P.O. Box 190, Arlington, Virginia 22210. When ordering, please specify the document number. Documents are available as noted in microfiche (MF) and paper copy (PC).

Adelman, Howard. 1973. *The Holiversity: A Perspective on the Wright Report*. Toronto: New Press.

Altbach, Philip G., and Berdahl, Robert O. 1981. *Higher Education in American Society*. Buffalo, N.Y.: Prometheus Books.

American Association of Community and Junior Colleges. Published annually. *Community, Junior, and Technical College Directory*. Washington, D.C.: American Association of Community and Junior Colleges.

American Association of State Colleges and Universities. Published monthly. *Connections*. Washington, D.C.: AASCU Publications.

———. 1981. *AASCU Policy Statements*. Washington, D.C.: American Association of State Colleges and Universities. ED 213 352. 11 pp. MF–$1.17; PC not available EDRS.

Ashby, Sir Eric. 1971. *Any Person, Any Study: An Essay on Higher Education in the United States*. New York: McGraw Hill.

Azaroff, Leonid V. 1982. "Industry-University Collaboration: How to Make It Work." *Research Management* 25(6).

Babbidge, Homer. 1968. "View from the Campus." In *Science Policy and the University*, edited by Harold Orlans. Washington, D.C.: The Brookings Institution.

Baer, Walter S. 1977. *University Relationships with Other R&D Performers*. Santa Monica, Calif.: The Rand Corporation. ED 144 468. 70 pp. MF–$1.17; PC–$7.24.

———. 1980. "Strengthening University-Industry Interactions." Santa Monica, Calif.: The Rand Corporation. ED 190 033. 30 pp. MF–$1.17; PC not available EDRS.

Banfield, Edward. 1970. *The Unheavenly City*. Boston: Little Brown.

Beasley, K., and Stauffer, T. c.1982. "Business–Higher Education Corporation on Research and Development: A Status Report."

Paper prepared for Business–Higher Education Forum. Mimeographed.

Bebout, John E. 1972. "The Emerging State Governments: A Challenge to Academia." In *The University and the Emerging Federalism: A Conference on Improving University Contributions to State Governments,* edited by S. K. Gove and E. K. Stewart. Urbana, Ill.: University of Illinois.

Berte, Neal R., and O'Neil, E. H. 1977. "Old and New Models of Service." In *Redefining Service, Research, and Teaching,* edited by Warren Bryan Martin. New Directions for Higher Education No. 18. San Francisco: Jossey-Bass.

Berube, Maurice R. 1978. *The Urban University in America.* Westport, Conn.: Greenwood Press.

Bickner, Robert E. 1972. "Science at the Service of Government: California Tries to Exploit an Unnatural Resource." *Policy Sciences* 3: 183–99.

Blocker, Clyde E.; Plummer, R. H.; and Richardson, R. C., Jr. 1965. *The Two-Year College: A Social Synthesis.* Englewood Cliffs, N.J.: Prentice Hall.

Bogue, Jesse P. 1950. *The Community College.* New York: McGraw Hill.

Bok, Derek. 1982. *Beyond the Ivory Tower: Social Responsibilities of the Modern University.* Cambridge: Harvard University Press.

Boulding, Kenneth E. 1975. "Truth or Power." *Science* 190:ii.

Bramlett, Gene A. 1974. *The Academic Community: A Backup Force to State Government.* A report to the National Science Foundation, Research Applied to National Needs. Atlanta: Southern Regional Education Board.

―――, ed. 1976. *University Services to State Government: Representative Approaches in Southern States.* Atlanta: Southern Regional Education Board. ED 132 918. 57 pp. MF–$1.17; PC–$7.24.

―――. 1979. "Some Generalizations about University Services to State Government." In *Linking Science and Technology to Public Policy: The Role of Universities,* edited by Abdo I. Baaklini. Albany, N.Y.: New York State Assembly and Comparative Development Studies Center, Graduate School of Public Affairs, SUNY–Albany.

Brawer, Florence B. 1980. "Familiar Functions in New Containers: Classifying Community Education." Topical Paper No. 71. Los Angeles: ERIC Clearinghouse for Junior College Information. ED 187 412. 30 pp. MF–$1.17; PC–$5.49.

Breneman, David W., and Nelson, Susan C. 1981. *Financing Community Colleges: An Economic Perspective.* Washington, D.C.: The Brookings Institution.

Brodsky, Neal H.; Kaufman, Harold G.; and Tooker, John D. 1980. *University-Industry Cooperation: A Preliminary Analysis of Existing Mechanisms and Their Relationship to the Innovation Process*. New York: New York University Graduate School of Public Administration, Center for Science and Technology Policy.

Brubacher, John S., and Rudy, Willis. 1976. *Higher Education in Transition*. 3d ed. New York: Harper & Row.

Carnegie Commission on Higher Education. 1970. *The Open-Door College*. New York: McGraw Hill.

———. 1972. *The Campus and the City*. New York: McGraw Hill.

Carnegie Foundation for the Advancement of Teaching. 1967. *The University at the Service of Society*. New York. ED 024 319. 14 pp. MF–$1.17; PC–$3.74.

Cohen, Arthur M. 1969. *Dateline '79: Heretical Concepts for the Community College*. Beverly Hills: Glencoe Press.

———. 1977. "Community Education, Social Equalization, and Other Whimseys." Paper presented at the Illinois Community College Presidents' Workshop, St. Charles, Ill. ED 139 479. 24 pp. MF–$1.17; PC–$3.74.

Cohen, Arthur M., and Associates. 1975. *College Responses to Community Demands*. San Francisco: Jossey-Bass.

Cohen, Arthur M., and Brawer, Florence B. 1982. *The American Community College*. San Francisco: Jossey-Bass.

Coldron, Sharon L., and others. 1981. *Data and Information Needs to Stimulate Effective College/City Cooperation for Community Development*. Washington, D.C.: American Council on Education. ED 208 756. 48 pp. MF–$1.17; PC–$5.49.

Commager, Henry Steele. 1978. "The College in American Education." In *The Past, Present, and Future of American Higher Education*, edited by Judyth L. Schaubhut. Washington, D.C.: Society for College and University Planning. ED 158 624. 51 pp. ME–$1.17; PC not available EDRS.

Cosand, Joseph P. 1981. "Perspectives: Community Education and Services in the 1980s." *Community Services Catalyst* 11(3): 4–8.

Council of State Governments. 1972. *Power to the States: Mobilizing Public Technology*. Lexington, Ky.: Council of State Governments.

Crittenden, Ann. 22 July 1981. "Industry's Role in Academia." *The New York Times*.

Cross, K. Patricia. 1982–83. "The Miami-Dade Breakthrough." In *Underprepared Learners*, edited by K. Patricia Cross. Current Issues in Education No. 1. Washington, D.C.: American Association for Higher Education.

Culliton, Barbara J. 1982a. "Academic-Industrial Complex." *Science* 216(4549): 960–63.

———. 1982b. "The Hoechst Department at Mass. General." *Science* 216(4551): 1200–1203.

———. 1982c. "Monsanto Gives Washington U. $23.5 Million." *Science* 216(4552): 1295–96.

David, Edward E. 1979. "Science Futures: The Industrial Connection." *Science* 203: 837–40.

———. 1982. "Striking a Bargain between Company and Campus." *Environment* 24(6): 42–45.

Dowling, Noreen G., and Stumbo, Diana. August 1981. "Public Service Research at University of California Davis." Paper presented at the annual meeting of the Rural Sociological Society. ED 209 986. 19 pp. MF–$1.17; PC not available EDRS.

Draper, Andrew S. 1907. "The American Type of University." *Science* 26: 33–43.

Dressel, Paul, and Faricy, William. 1972. *Return to Responsibility*. San Francisco: Jossey-Bass.

Drucker, Peter S. 1979. "Science and Industry: Challenges of Antagonistic Interdependence." *Science* 204: 806–10.

Eddy, Edward D., Jr. 1957. *Colleges for Our Land and Time*. New York: Harper.

Eells, W. C. 1931. *The Junior College*. Boston: Houghton Mifflin.

Eliot, Charles William. 1869. "The New Education." *Atlantic Monthly* 23: 203–20, 358–67.

Eulau, Heinz, and Quinley, Harold. 1970. *State Officials and Higher Education*. New York: McGraw Hill.

Everett, Edward. 1848. "On Harvard's Need for State Funds, 1848–49." In *American Higher Education: A Documentary History,* vol. 1, edited by Richard Hofstader and Wilson Smith. Chicago: University of Chicago Press, 1961.

Feller, Irwin. 1979. "Interim Observations, Reservations, and Other Cautionary Comments about University Assistance to State Governments." In *Linking Science and Technology to Public Policy: The Role of Universities,* edited by Abdo I. Baaklini. Albany, N.Y.: New York State Assembly and Comparative Development Studies Center, Graduate School of Public Affairs, SUNY–Albany.

Feller, I.; King, M. R.; Mentzel, D.C.; O'Conner, R. E.; and Wissel, P. A. 1975. *Sources and Uses of Scientific and Technological Information in State Legislatures*. University Park, Pa.: The Pennsylvania State University Institute for Research on Human Resources.

Flexner, Abraham. 1930. "Abraham Flexner Criticizes the American University, 1930." In *American Higher Education: A*

Documentary History, vol. 1, edited by Richard Hofstader and Wilson Smith. Chicago: University of Chicago Press, 1961.

Folger, John. 1980. "Implications of State Government Changes." In *Improving Academic Management,* edited by Paul Jedamus, Marvin W. Peterson, and associates. San Francisco: Jossey-Bass.

Fusfeld, Herbert I. 1976. "Industry-University R&D: New Approaches to Support and Working Relationships." *Research Management* 19(3): 21–24.

———. 1980. "The Bridge between University and Industry." *Science* 209(4453): 221–23.

Garnett, James L. 1979. "Strategies for Governors Who Want to Reorganize." *State Government* 52(3): 135–43.

Geiger, Louis G. 1963. *Higher Education in a Maturing Democracy.* Lincoln: University of Nebraska Press.

Giamatti, A. Bartlett. 1981. *The University and the Public Interest.* New York: Atheneum.

Gilder, Jamison, and Rocha, Jessica. 1980. "10,000 Cooperative Arrangements Serve 1.5 Million." *Community and Junior College Journal* 51(3): 11–17.

Gilman, Daniel C. 1872. "The University of California in Its Infancy." In *University Problems in the United States.* New York: Arno Press and The New York Times, 1969.

Gleazer, Edmund J., Jr. 1974a. "After the Boom . . . What Now for the Community Colleges?" *Community and Junior College Journal* 44(4): 6–11.

———. 1974b. "Beyond the Open Door: The Open College." *Community and Junior College Journal* 45(1): 6–12.

———. 1980. *The Community College: Values, Vision, and Vitality.* Washington, D.C.: American Association of Community and Junior Colleges. ED 187 364. 197 pp. MF–$1.17; PC not available EDRS.

Gollattscheck, James F.; Harlacher, E. L.; Roberts, E.; and Wygal, B. R. 1976. *College Leadership for Community Renewal.* San Francisco: Jossey-Bass.

Goodall, Leonard E., ed. 1976. *State Politics and Higher Education.* Dearborn, Mich.: UMG Associates.

Gove, Samuel K. 1979. "State Government–University Relations: The Illinois Experience." In *Linking Science and Technology to Public Policy: The Role of Universities,* edited by Abdo I. Baaklini. Albany, N.Y.: New York State Assembly and Comparative Development Studies Center, Graduate School of Public Affairs, SUNY–Albany.

Gove, Samuel A., and Stewart, Elizabeth K., eds. 1972. *The University and the Emerging Federalism: A Conference on*

Improving University Contributions to State Government.
Urbana, Ill.: University of Illinois.

Harlacher, Ervin L. 1969. *The Community Dimension of the Community College.* Englewood Cliffs, N.J.: Prentice Hall.

Harper, William A. 1977. *Community, Junior, and Technical Colleges: A Public Relations Sourcebook.* Washington, D.C.: Hemisphere Publishing Co.

Henderson, Algo D. 1968. "Colleges and Universities As Agents of Social Change: An Introduction." In *Colleges and Universities As Agents of Social Change,* edited by W. John Minter and Ian M. Thompson. Berkeley, Calif.: Center for Research and Development in Higher Education, University of California, Berkeley. ED 144 503. 156 pp. ME–$1.17; PC–$15.01.

Henry, Nicholas. 1976. "State Agencies and Academia." *State Government* 49(2): 99–104.

Hofstader, Richard, and Smith, Wilson, eds. 1961. *American Higher Education: A Documentary History.* Chicago: University of Chicago Press.

Hollinshead, B. S. 1936. "The Community Junior College Program." *Junior College Journal* 7(3): 111–16.

Huber, James H. 1975. "Urban Studies: An Opportunity for Synthesis among Social Policy Sciences." *Intellect* 104(2369): 162–65.

Hutchins, Robert M. 1936. *The Higher Learning in America.* New Haven: Yale University Press.

Ikenberry, Stanley O., and Friedman, R. C. 1972. *Beyond Academic Departments.* San Francisco: Jossey-Bass.

Institute of Government and Public Affairs. 1983. "Faculty Research Assistance to the State (FRATS)." Mimeographed. Urbana, Ill.: Institute of Government and Public Affairs, University of Illinois.

Institute of Governmental Studies. 1982. *California Policy Seminar Annual Report.* Berkeley, Calif.: Institute of Governmental Studies, University of California, Berkeley.

James, Edmund J. 1905. "The Function of the State University." *Science* 22: 609–28.

Johnson, Jerald. 1968. "The University as Problem Solver: Creativity and the Ghetto." *Liberal Education* 54(3): 418–28.

Jones, Robert G. 1979. "Linking Research to the Development of State Public Policy: Illustrations and Perspective from a Multicampus University." In *Linking Science and Technology to Public Policy: The Role of Universities,* edited by Abdo I. Baaklini. Albany, N.Y.: New York State Assembly and Comparative Development Studies Center, Graduate School of Public Affairs, SUNY–Albany.

Kavanaugh, L. 1979. "Community Service: The Future of Community Colleges." *Educational Record* 60(2): 202–6.

Kaysen, Carl. 1969. *The Higher Learning, the Universities, and the Public*. Princeton: Princeton University Press.

Keim, William A. 1976. "A Dynamic Definition of Service." In *Reaching out through Community Service,* edited by H. M. Holcomb. New Directions for Community Colleges No. 14. San Francisco: Jossey-Bass.

Kerr, Clark. 1972. *The Uses of the University—with a Postscript— 1972*. Cambridge: Harvard University Press.

Kerr, W. J. 1961. *The Spirit of the Land-Grant Institutions*. Tucson: University of Arizona Press.

Kiefer, David M. 1980. "Forging New and Stronger Links between University and Industrial Scientists." *Chemical and Engineering News* 58(49): 38–51.

Kimsky, Sheldon. 1982. "The University: Marketing Theories, not Toothpaste." *Environment* 24(6): 46–48.

Kolbe, Parke D. 1928. *Urban Influences on Higher Education in England and the United States*. New York: Macmillan Co.

Koos, L. V. 1925. *The Junior-College Movement*. New York: Ginn & Co.

Latker, Norman J. 1977. "University Patent Policy." Paper presented at annual Academic Planning Conference, University of Southern California, Los Angeles. ED 138 170. 13 pp. MF–$1.17; PC–$3.74.

Leo, Robert J. 1977. "The Colleges' Roles for Science." In *Redefining Service, Research, and Teaching,* edited by Warren Bryan Martin. New Directions for Higher Education No. 18. San Francisco: Jossey-Bass.

Libsch, Joseph F. 1976. "Industry-University R&D: The Role of the Small, High Technology University." *Research Management* 19(3): 28–31.

Lindblom, Charles E., and Cohen, David K. 1979. *Usable Knowledge: Social Science and Social Problem Solving*. New Haven: Yale University Press.

Lombardi, John. 1978. "Community Education: Threat to College Status?" Topical Paper No. 68. Los Angeles: ERIC Clearinghouse for Junior College Information. ED 156 296. 45 pp. MF–$1.17; PC–$5.49.

Long, Norton E., and Groskind, N. E. 1972. "Updating the Land Grant Tradition." *Change* 4: 6–7, 69.

Lowi, Theodore J. 1970. "Higher Education: A Political Analysis." *Liberal Education* 56: 238–53.

Luria, S. E., and Luria, Zella. 1970. "The Role of the University: Ivory Tower, Service Station, or Frontier Post?" *Daedalus* 99(1): 75–83.

Lusterman, Seymour. 1977. *Education in Industry: A Research Report from the Conference Board's Public Affairs Research Division*. New York: The Conference Board.

Lynton, Ernest A. 1982. "Corporate Education: College Opportunity." *AGB Reports* 24(1): 42–46.

———. Forthcoming. *The Missing Connection between Business and Education*. New York: Macmillan Co.

McNeil, Donald. 1974. "Synthesis." *National Conference on Public Service and Extension in Institutions of Higher Education*. Athens, Ga.: University of Georgia. ED 098 856. 122 pp. MF–$1.17; PC not available EDRS.

Martin, Warren Bryan. 1977. "Service through Ideas of Value." In *Redefining Service, Research, and Teaching*, edited by Warren Bryan Martin. New Directions for Higher Education No. 18. San Francisco: Jossey-Bass.

———. 1982. "What Universities Do That Nobody Else Can." *AGB Reports* 24: 57–63.

Mather, Anne D. 1976. "How Colleges Can Help State Governments." *AGB Reports* 18(2): 8–10.

Mayville, William V. 1980. "Changing Perspectives on the Urban College and University." AAHE/ERIC Higher Education Research Currents. Washington, D.C.: ERIC Clearinghouse on Higher Education. ED 185 890. 5 pp. MF–$1.17; PC–$3.74.

Miller, Lorna M., ed. 1980. *Community Service and Continuing Education: Program Abstracts*. 2d ed. Madison: Wisconsin University Extension. ED 192 120. 803 pp. MF–$1.97; PC not available EDRS.

Minter, W. John, and Thompson, Ian M. eds. 1968. *Colleges and Universities as Agents of Social Change*. Berkeley, Calif.: Center for Research and Development in Higher Education, University of California–Berkeley. ED 144 503. 156 pp. MF–$1.17; PC–$15.01.

Murray, Michael A. 1975. "The State, Academia, and Cooperative Research." *Planning and Changing* 5(4): 238–45.

Myran, Gunder A. 1969. *Community Services in the Community College*. Washington, D.C.: American Association of Junior Colleges. ED 037 202. 60 pp. MF–$1.17; PC–$7.24.

———. 1974. "Community Services: Issues, Challenges, and Perspective." In *Beyond the Open Door, the Open College: A Report on the National Conference on Community Services and the Community College*. Orlando, Fla.: Valencia Community College.

———. 1978a. "Antecedents: Evolution of the Community-Based College." In *Implementing Community-Based Education*, edited by E. L. Harlacher and J. F. Gollattscheck. New Directions for Community Colleges No. 21. San Francisco: Jossey-Bass.

———. 1978b. "Community Services in Small/Rural Community Colleges: A Role in Rural Development." Paper presented at the National Conference on Small/Rural Colleges, Blacksburg, Virginia. ED 165 844. 10 pp. MF–$1.17; PC–$3.74.

National Commission on Research. 1980. *Industry and the Universities: Developing Cooperative Research Relationships in the National Interest*. Washington, D. C.: National Commission on Research.

National Council on Community Services and Continuing Education. Published monthly. *Community Services Catalyst*. Blacksburg, Va.: National Council on Community Services and Continuing Education, College of Education, Virginia Polytechnic Institute and State University.

National Science Foundation. 1982. "Academic R&D Expenditures Increased 4% in Real Terms between FY1979 and FY1980, but Leveled in FY1981." *Science Resources Studies Highlights* NSF–309.

———. 1983. *Guide to Programs*. Washington, D.C.: National Science Foundation.

Nevins, Alan. 1962. *The State Universities and Democracy*. Urbana, Ill.: University of Illinois Press.

Nickens, John M. 1976. "A Taxonomy for Community Services." In *Reaching out through Community Service*, edited by H. M. Holcomb. New Directions for Community Colleges No. 14. San Francisco: Jossey-Bass.

Noble, David S. 1977. *American by Design: Science, Technology, and the Rise of Corporate Capitalism*. New York: Alfred A. Knopf.

Noble, David S., and Pfund, Nancy E. 1980. "Business Goes Back to College." *The Nation* 231: 233.

Omenn, Gilbert. 1982. "Reenergizing the Research University." *Environment* 24(6): 49–51.

Orlans, Harold, ed. 1968. *Science Policy and the University*. Washington, D.C.: The Brookings Institution.

Pajaro Dunes Conference. 1982. "Draft Statement." Mimeographed.

Palmer, James C. 1981. "Managing Community Services Programs." *Community Services Catalyst* 11(3): 26–29.

Parsons, Talcott, and Platt, Gerald M. 1973. *The American University*. Cambridge: Harvard University Press.

Pendleton, William C. 1974. "Urban Studies and the University: The Ford Foundation Experience." New York: Ford Foundation. ED 097 857. 10 pp. MF–$1.17; PC–$3.74.

Penniman, Clara. 1979. "Seventy-Five Years of State Government Collaboration." In *Linking Science and Technology to Public Policy: The Role of Universities,* edited by Abdo I. Baaklini. Albany, N.Y.: New York State Assembly and Comparative Development Studies Center, Graduate School of Public Affairs, SUNY–Albany.

Phillips, Ione. 1977. *The Added Dimension: State and Land Grant Universities Serving State and Local Government.* Washington, D.C.: National Association of State Universities and Land Grant Colleges. ED 136 720. 175 pp. MF–$1.17; PC–$15.01.

Pifer, Alan. 1974. "Community College and Community Leadership." *Community and Junior College Journal* 44(8): 23–26.

Prager, Denis J., and Omenn, Gilbert S. 1980. "Research, Innovation, and University-Industry Linkages." *Science* 207: 379–84.

Riley, George; Baldridge, J. Victor; and others. 1978. *Policy Making and Effective Leadership.* San Francisco: Jossey-Bass.

Rosenzweig, Robert M. 1982. *The Research Universities and Their Patrons.* Berkeley, Calif.: University of California Press.

Roy, Rustum. 1972. "University-Industry Interaction Patterns." *Science* 178: 955–60.

Rudolph, Frederick. 1962. *The American College and University.* New York: Alfred A. Knopf.

Sanchez, Bonnie, compiler. 1977. "About Community College Community Education and Community Services: A 'Brief' Highlighting Important Literature since 1965 about Community Education and Community Services in the Community College." Los Angeles: ERIC Clearinghouse for Junior College Information. ED 140 927. 23 pp. MF–$1.17; PC–$3.74.

Schneider, Mark, and Swinton, David. 1979. "A Symposium: Policy Analysis in State and Local Government." *Public Administration Review* 39(1): 12–16.

Scott, Robert W. 1974. "State Government as a Client for Public Service and Extension Activities." In *National Conference on Public Service and Extension in Institutions of Higher Education.* Washington, D.C.: National Association of State Universities and Land-Grant Colleges. ED 098 856. 122 pp. MF–$1.17; PC not available EDRS.

Shroyer, David L. 1980. "Assisting Students to Succeed in Higher Education." *Connections* 2(1): 2–4. ED 187 271.

Silber, John R. 1976. "Financing the Independent Sector." In *Current Issues in Higher Education,* edited by Dyckman W. Vermilye. Washington, D.C.: American Association for Higher Education.

———. 1978. "Monopoly, Diversity, and Opportunity." In *The*

Past, Present, and Future of American Higher Education,
edited by Judyth L. Schaubhut. Washington, D.C.: Society for
College and University Planning. ED 158 624. 51 pp. MF–$1.17;
PC not available EDRS.

Slosson, Edwin E. 1910. *Great American Universities.* New York:
Macmillan Co.

Smith, Bruce L. R., and Karlesky, Joseph J., eds. 1978a. *The
State of Academic Science: Background Papers.* New York:
Change Magazine Press.

———. 1978b. *The State of Academic Science: The Universities in
the Nation's Research Effort.* New York: Change Magazine
Press.

Smith, Hayden W. c.1982a. "Corporate Support of Higher
Education: A Position Statement." Paper prepared for the
January 1983 meeting of the Business–Higher Education Forum.
Mimeographed.

———. c.1982b. "Corporate-University Relations: A Proposed
Action Agenda." Paper prepared for the January 1983 meeting
of the Business–Higher Education Forum. Mimeographed.

Solo, Robert A. 1975. *Organizing Science for Technology Transfer
in Economic Development.* East Lansing. Mich.: Michigan
State University Press.

Southern Regional Education Board. 1975. "The Community
College and Its Community Service Role." Issues in Higher
Education No. 8. Atlanta: Southern Regional Education Board.
ED 148 420. 8 pp. MF–$1.17; PC–$3.74.

State University of New York. 1978. *The Third Dimension: Public
Services of the State University of New York.* Albany, N.Y.:
State University Office of Public Service, State University of
New York.

State University System of Florida. 1982. "Service through the
Application of Research." Mimeographed. Tallahassee:
Institute of Government, Florida State University.

Steffens, Lincoln. 1909. "What the University of Wisconsin Is
Doing for Its People." In *Portraits of the American University,*
compiled by James Stone and Donald DeNevi. San Francisco:
Jossey-Bass, 1971.

Thomas, Robert C., and Ruffner, James A. 1982. *Research
Centers Directory* and *New Research Centers.* 7th ed. Detroit:
Gale Research Company.

Touraine, Alain. 1974. *The American System in American Society.*
New York: McGraw Hill.

Trow, Martin A. 1982–83. "Underprepared Students at Public
Research Universities." In *Underprepared Learners,* edited by
K. Patricia Cross. Current Issues in Education No. 1. Washing-
ton, D.C.: American Association for Higher Education.

Tuckman, Howard P. 1976. *Publication, Teaching, and the Academic Reward Structure*. Lexington, Mass.: Lexington Books.

Turner, Jonathan Baldwin. 1851. "Plan for an Industrial University for the State of Illinois." In *The Colleges and the Public, 1787–1862,* edited by Theodore R. Crane. New York: Teachers College, Columbia University, 1963.

University of California. 1974. *Applied and Public Service Research in the University of California: Proceedings of the University of California's 28th Annual Faculty Conference*. Berkeley, Calif.: University of California.

University of Massachusetts. 1971. *President's Committee on the Future of the University Report*. Boston: University of Massachusetts Central Administration.

University of Pittsburgh. 1982. "Applied Science and Technology at the University of Pittsburgh." Mimeographed. Pittsburgh: Center for Applied Science and Technology, University of Pittsburgh.

Van Hise, Charles R. 1910. "The University and the State." *American Education Review* 31: 677–78.

Vaughan, George Brandt. 1980. "Community Services and the Community College: Reestablishing the Mission." *Community Services Catalyst* 11(2): 4–10.

Veblen, Thorstein. 1957. *The Higher Learning in America*. New York: A. M. Kelley.

Veysey, Laurence R. 1965. *The Emergence of the American University*. Chicago: University of Chicago Press.

Weiss, Carol. 1979. "The Many Meanings of Research Utilization." *Public Administration Review* 39(5): 426–31.

Wilson, Woodrow. 1896. "Princeton in the Nation's Service." In *American Higher Education: A Documentary History,* vol. 2, edited by Richard Hofstader and Wilson Smith. Chicago: University of Chicago Press, 1961.

Wofford, Harris L. 1968. "Agents of Whom." In *Colleges and Universities as Agents of Social Change,* edited by W. John Minter and Ian M. Thompson. Berkeley, Calif: Center for Research and Development in Higher Education, University of California–Berkeley. ED 144 503. 156 pp. MF–$1.17; PC–$15.01.

Wolff, Robert Paul. 1969. *The Ideal of the University*. Boston: Beacon Press.

Wolfle, Dael. 1972. *The Home of Science: The Role of the University*. New York: McGraw Hill.

Worthley, John A., and Apfel, Jeffrey. 1978. "University Assistance to State Government." *Journal of Higher Education* 49(6): 608–19.

Wright, Deil S.; Wagner, Mary; and McAnaw, Richard. 1977. "State Administrators: Their Changing Characteristics." *State Government* 50(3): 152–59.

Wygal, Benjamin R. 1981. "Community Services: Organizational Concepts Revisited." *Community Services Catalyst* 11(4): 3–7.

Yarrington, Roger. 1974. "An Interview with Ervin Harlacher: What Does It Mean to Be Community-Based?" *Community and Junior College Journal* 45(1): 13–18.

———. 1976. "Finding the Funds." In *Reaching out through Community Service,* edited by H. M. Holcomb. New Directions for Community Colleges No. 14. San Francisco: Jossey-Bass.

———. 1980. "Interpreting the Mission." *Community and Junior College Journal* 51(2): 6–10.

Young, Robert B.; Fletcher, Suzanne M.; and Rue, Robert R. 1978. *Directions for the Future: An Analysis of the Community Services Dimension of Community Colleges.* Community Education Monograph No. 2. Washington, D. C.: National Center for Community Education, American Association of Community and Junior Colleges; and Ann Arbor, Mich.: Office of Community Education Research, University of Michigan. ED 158 787. 70 pp. MC–$1.17; PC–$7.24.

Zollinger, Richard. 1982. "State-sponsored Research: Cooperation or Conflict?" *Educational Record* 63(1): 4–9.

ASHE-ERIC HIGHER EDUCATION
RESEARCH REPORTS

Starting in 1983, the Association for the Study of Higher Education assumed co-sponsorship of the Higher Education Research Reports with the ERIC Clearinghouse on Higher Education. For the previous 11 years, ERIC and the American Association for Higher Education prepared and published the reports.

Each report is the definitive analysis of a tough higher education problem, based on a thorough research of pertinent literature and institutional experiences. Report topics, identified by a national survey, are written by noted practitioners and scholars with prepublication manuscript reviews by experts.

Ten monographs in the ASHE-ERIC/Higher Education Research Report series are published each year, available individually or by subscription. Subscription to 10 issues is $50 regular; $35 for members of AERA, AAHE, and AIR; $30 for members of ASHE. (Add $7.50 outside U.S.)

Prices for single copies, including 4th class postage and handling, are $6.50 regular and $5.00 for members of AERA, AAHE, AIR, and ASHE. If faster first-class postage is desired for U.S. and Canadian orders, for each publication ordered add $.60; for overseas, add $4.50. For VISA and MasterCard payments, give card number, expiration date, and signature. Orders under $25 must be prepaid. Bulk discounts are available on orders of 10 or more of a single title. Order from the Publications Department, Association for the Study of Higher Education, One Dupont Circle, Suite 630, Washington, D.C. 20036, (202) 296-2597. Write for a complete list of Higher Education Research Reports and other ASHE and ERIC publications.

1981 Higher Education Research Reports

1. Minority Access to Higher Education
   Jean L. Preer

2. Institutional Advancement Strategies in Hard Times
   Michael D. Richards and Gerald Sherratt

3. Functional Literacy in the College Setting
   Richard C. Richardson, Jr., Kathryn J. Martens, and Elizabeth C. Fisk

4. Indices of Quality in the Undergraduate Experience
   George D. Kuh

5. Marketing in Higher Education
   Stanley M. Grabowski

6. Computer Literacy in Higher Education
   Francis E. Masat

7. Financial Analysis for Academic Units
   Donald L. Walters

8. Assessing the Impact of Faculty Collective Bargaining
   J. Victor Baldridge, Frank R. Kemerer, and Associates

9. Strategic Planning, Management, and Decision Making
    Robert G. Cope
10. Organizational Communication in Higher Education
    Robert D. Gratz and Philip J. Salem

1982 Higher Education Research Reports

1. Rating College Teaching: Criterion Studies of Student
   Evaluation-of-Instruction Instruments
   Sidney E. Benton
2. Faculty Evaluation: The Use of Explicit Criteria for
   Promotion, Retention, and Tenure
   Neal Whitman and Elaine Weiss
3. The Enrollment Crisis: Factors, Actors, and Impacts
   *J. Victor Baldridge, Frank R. Kemerer, and Kenneth C.
   Green*
4. Improving Instruction: Issues and Alternatives for Higher
   Education
   Charles C. Cole, Jr.
5. Planning for Program Discontinuance: From Default to Design
   Gerlinda S. Melchiori
6. State Planning, Budgeting, and Accountability: Approaches
   for Higher Education
   Carol E. Floyd
7. The Process of Change in Higher Education Institutions
   Robert C. Nordvall
8. Information Systems and Technological Decisions: A Guide
   for Non-Technical Administrators
   Robert L. Bailey
9. Government Support for Minority Participation in Higher
   Education
   Kenneth C. Green
10. The Department Chair: Professional Development and Role
    Conflict
    David B. Booth

1983 Higher Education Research Reports

1. The Path to Excellence: Quality Assurance in Higher
   Education
   *Laurence R. Marcus, Anita O. Leone, and Edward D.
   Goldberg*
2. Faculty Recruitment, Retention and Fair Employment:
   Obligations and Opportunities
   John S. Waggaman
3. The Crisis in Faculty Careers: Changes and Challenges
   Michael C. T. Brookes and Katherine L. German